THE CATHOLIC UNIVERSITY OF AMERICA
CANON LAW STUDIES
No. 330

THE CESSATION OF DELEGATED POWER

A CANONICAL COMMENTARY
WITH HISTORICAL NOTES

by

THE REVEREND MAX GEORGE DEWITT, A.B., J.C.L.
Priest of the Diocese of Lincoln

A DISSERTATION

Submitted to the Faculty of the School of Canon Law of the Catholic University of America in Partial Fulfillment of the Requirements for the Degree of Doctor of Canon Law

THE CATHOLIC UNIVERSITY OF AMERICA PRESS
WASHINGTON, D. C.
1954

NIHIL OBSTAT:
JOANNES ROGG SCHMIDT, A.B., J.C.D.
Censor Deputatus

Washingtonii, D.C., die 16 Septembris 1953

IMPRIMATUR:
✠ LUDOVICUS BENEDICTUS KUCERA, D.D.
Episcopus Lincolnensis

Lincolniae, die 26 Septembris 1953

Printed by The Abbey Press, St. Meinrad, Indiana

DEDICATED

to the late

RT. REV. MSGR. H. LOUIS MOTRY, S.T.D., J.C.D.

Dean of the School of Canon Law

* * * * *

A WORTHY PRIEST

AND

A LOYAL FRIEND OF PRIESTS

TABLE OF CONTENTS

FOREWORD

The Church founded by our Divine Savior is, by its nature and in its own right, a juridically perfect supernatural society whose end is the sanctification and the salvation of its members. Such a perfect society must be endowed with the authoritative power to accomplish its end. Christ Himself established in His Church this authoritative power, or the power to rule, in the jurisdictional offices of the supreme pontificate and the subordinate episcopate.[1] Through these the public good of the whole society of the Church and the private good of the individual members of the Church is to be attained.

The seed of the Church has gradually come to possess the stature of a huge tree whose branches shadow the entire earth. As this society flourished and continues to grow, its constituted authority utilizes every good means in order to more expeditiously accomplish the *raison d'être* of the Church. From earliest times this authority recognized the impossibility of personally attending to every detail, and thus found it necessary in practice to act through others. Even the Apostles did not hesitate to extend their effectiveness in this manner.[2] Just as delegation or acting through a substitute was the natural solution for the Apostles, so it has remained a solution throughout the history of the Church. The incorporation of the vital institute of delegation in the present legal system of the Church is explicit.

But precisely because delegated power is substituted or representative power it must be carefully examined, lest,

[1] Eugene IV (in conc. Floren.), const. *Laetentur coeli,* 6 iulii 1439, n. 8—*Codicis Iuris Canonici Fontes,* cura Emi Petri Card. Gasparri editi (9 vols., Romae (postea Civitate Vaticana): Typis Polyglottis Vaticanis, 1923-1939. Vols. VII-IX, ed. cura et studio Emi Iustiniani Card. Serédi), n. 51 (hereafter cited as *Fontes*); Leo XIII, ep. encycl. *Satis cognitum,* 29 iun. 1896, §§ 13, 19—*Fontes,* n. 630.

[2] Cf. Titus, I, 5; III, 12; I Cor., IV, 17.

in fact, there be misrepresentation or possibly no substitution at all. The present work is proposed as such a study, but with certain restrictions. It is beyond the pale of this work to examine every possible facet of delegation, or even to give a general treatment of the principles of delegation. The latter has already been accomplished in a fine study entitled *The Principles of Delegation* by the Reverend Raymond A. Kearney, A.B., S.T.D., J.C.D., to whom the present writer feels obliged to express his indebtedness and gratitude. The present work intends to expand and supplement Chapter VIII, *The Cessation of Delegation,* of this earlier dissertation of the Catholic University of America Canon Law Studies.

The direct object of this present work is to examine the various means which effect the cessation of delegated power. Only incidentally, and in so far as he judges it necessary, will the writer go beyond this direct object. Therefore, beyond the scope of this work are such questions as, how is valid delegation made, or what are the limits of delegating. Moreover of direct concern here is the extinction of delegated *jurisdictional* power, although throughout this work the term "delegated power" or "delegation" alone is used.

In order to present the subject matter in its proper conspectus, it was deemed advisable to present a summary consideration of the notion of jurisdiction in Roman Law and Canon Law, and also the notion of delegation according to both. Then the remainder of the work is devoted to the subject matter in hand.

It will be noticed that a historical development relative to the cessation of delegated power is not given a separate part in this work. It was decided that greater advantage could result through a presentation of the historical basis for the present legislation in conjunction with each article of the present law, rather than as a separate part. This procedure is especially preferred because of the nature of the subject. Each of the articles is a distinct subject, which for the most part has suffered no change since the earliest legislation of the Church.

It is difficult to reckon, and therefore to acknowledge, the various factors that have contributed to the fruition of the writer's efforts. Some factors or influences have been passing and accidental, while others were substantial and persistent. All of these, whether known or unknown to the writer, stand in his gratitude. In particular the writer wishes to express his gratitude to His Excellency, The Most Reverend Louis B. Kucera, D.D., Bishop of Lincoln, for the opportunity of pursuing the study of Canon Law. Also this gratitude is extended to the entire Faculty of the School of Canon Law at the Catholic University of America. Not to be forgotten, and much less to be underestimated, are the members of the School of Canon Law who, by discussion and encouragement, have greatly assisted in bringing this work to completion.

PART ONE

THE CONCEPT OF DELEGATION

CHAPTER I

PRELIMINARY NOTIONS

An examination of the nature of society not only indicates four essential elements, namely, members, the bond of union, the end and the means, but also distinctly points to the necessity of authority,[1] which, to say the least, is a *conditio sine qua non* for the existence of any society.[2] This principle of authority is the power of obligating the members of society, so that they may cooperate in the common goal.[3] That the Church is possessed of such power is evidenced by the fact that it is constituted as a juridically perfect supernatural society,[4] and as such has adequate power to attain its end. Consequently the Church has been endowed by Christ, not only with the power of orders,[5] but also with the power of jurisdiction.[6] This power of jurisdiction, as Ottaviani says, is that which the Church has for governing men, that is, for authoritatively directing their acts both with regard to faith and with regard to morals.[7] The Code of Canon Law summarily expresses this same notion with the words "*potestas regiminis.*"[8]

[1] Ottaviani, *Institutiones Iuris Publici Ecclesiastici* (3. ed., 2 vols., Romae: Typis Polyglottis Vaticanis, 1947-1948), I, nn. 15-18 (hereafter cited Ottaviani).

[2] Leo XIII, litt. encycl. *Immortale Dei*, 1 nov. 1885—*Acta Sanctae Sedis* (41 vols., Romae, 1865-1908), XVIII (1885), 165.

[3] St. Thomas, *De Regimine Principum* (Vivès ed., Vol. XXVII), lib. I, c. I; Ottaviani, I, n. 28.

[4] Pius XI, litt. encycl. *Divini illius magistri*, 3 dec. 1929—*Acta Apostolicae Sedis, Commentarium Officiale* (Romae, 1909—), XXII (1930), 52-53 (hereafter cited *AAS*).

[5] Canon 947.

[6] Canon 196.

[7] Ottaviani, I, n. 112, p. 199.

[8] Canon 196.

Unfortunately in the course of legal history the word *jurisdiction* did not always convey the same meaning that it does today. That this may be duly pointed out, the word will be explained according to Roman Law and Canon Law usage.

Article 1. Notion of Jurisdiction in Roman Law

Just as it is impossible to abstract a single canon from the Code of Canon Law and give it an adequately clear explanation independent of and unrelated to other sections of the Code, so it is equally impossible to grasp the Roman Law notion of jurisdiction without a general understanding of the governmental structure of Roman society and also the procedural systems for administering justice.

In Roman Law the governmental structure or the power of ruling was distinguished into four grades, namely, *maiestas, imperium, iurisdictio* and *notio.*[9] *Maiestas* was the greatest power, and, indeed, the foundation of all power. Sanguinetti (1829-1893) referred to this as equivalent to legislative power, which ultimately resided in the Roman populace, though exercised through different agencies at different times.[10] *Imperium* was the power which belonged

[9] Sanguinetti, *Iuris Ecclesiastici Institutiones* (3. ed., Romae, 1896), p. 233 (hereafter cited Sanguinetti).

[10] Sanguinetti, *loc. cit.* In the regal period, *maiestas* was vested in the King who was the sole authority. —D. (1. 2) (2. 1). For detailed description cf. Wenger, *Institutes of the Roman Law of Civil Procedure* (revised ed., translated by Otis Harrison Fisk, New York: Veritas Press, 1940), p. 38 (hereafter cited Wenger); Cumin, *A Manual of Civil Law* (2. ed., London, 1865), pp. 1-2 (hereafter cited Cumin); Sohm, *The Institutes, a Text-Book of the History and System of Roman Private Law* (3. ed., translated by James Ledlie, Oxford, 1907), pp. 34-42 (hereafter cited Sohm). At the commencement of the 5th century B.C., the *comitiae* had rebelled against the King and established a republic with a senate and two consuls in authority. —D. (1. 2) 2. 3, 16. Cf. Sherman, *Roman Law in the Modern World* (2. ed., 3 vols., New York, 1924), II, 430; Wenger, p. 54. Then in about the year 27 B.C. the Empire was inaugurated under Augustus, and authority passed to the Emperor.—Cf. Voet, *Ad Pandectas* (5. ed., 7 vols. in 4, Bassani, 1827), Lib. I, Tit. IV, n. 1 (hereafter cited Voet).

to superior magistrates. It included the power of judging in criminal cases and of inflicting penalties, even the extreme penalty of death and of granting possession of goods.[11] This is synonymous with what today is called coactive power,[12] and was called mere *imperium.*[13] Mixed *imperium,* which included jurisdiction, was the power that belonged to a magistrate by which he heard civil cases.[14] This notion of jurisdiction will be considered further. *Iurisdictio* admittedly has received various interpretations by Roman Law commentators, but always it has reference to judicial matters.[15]

The meaning of jurisdiction in Roman Law is taken from the etymology of the word and technically has a restricted meaning. As the composition of the word indicates, it is the *potestas iuris dicendi* and signifies the power to declare what is just.[16] Consequently it has been defined by the Glossators to the *Digest* as the power publicly introduced with the right of declaring what is just and stating what is equitable.[17] Hence jurisdiction in Roman Law means only

[11] D. (2. 1) 3. Cf. Maroto, *Institutiones Iuris Canonici,* Tomus I (3. ed., Romae, 1921), n. 573, in nota 1, p. 660 (hereafter cited Maroto).

[12] Sanguinetti, p. 234.

[13] Maroto, I, n. 573, in nota 1, p. 660. Cf. also Donellus (Hugues Doneau), *Opera Omnia* (12 vols., Romae et Maceratae, 1828-1833), IV, lib. XVII, cap. VI, n. I (hereafter cited Donellus); Voet, Lib. II, Tit. I, n. 43.

[14] Maroto, I, n. 573, in nota 1, p. 660.

[15] Voet, Lib. II, Tit. I, n. 1; Donellus, IV, lib. XVII, cap. VI, n. V, in nota 6; Kearney, *The Principles of Delegation,* The Catholic University of America Canon Law Studies, n. 55 (Washington, D. C.: The Catholic University of America, 1929), p. 45 (hereafter cited Kearney). The evolution of the meaning of the word "jurisdiction" in Roman Law is concisely explained by Van de Kerckhove. —"De Notione Jurisdictionis in Jure Romano," *Jus Pontificium* (Romae, 1921-1940), XVI (1936), 49-65.

[16] Donellus, IV, lib. XVII, cap. VI, n. V.

[17] *Glossa,* introd. ad D. (2. 1)—"... iurisdictio in genere sumpta, potestas de publico introducta, cum necessitate iuris dicendi, et aequitatis statuendae.... Et dicitur... a iuris et ditione."—*Digestum Vetus,* Digestorum seu Pandectarum Iuris Enucleati, adiecimus huic

the power or authority of taking cognizance of a cause, of judging, of executing the sentence and of giving or nominating a judge, and does not *per se* include coercive power, much less legislative.[18] Perez defined jurisdiction as the *publica de causis cognoscendi et iudicandi potestas* without including the right to execute the sentence.[19] Nevertheless authors generally conceded that the power of executing the sentence was, if not a part of jurisdiction itself, at least a necessary condition for its proper use.[20]

The word *notio* also occurs in a consideration of the meaning of jurisdiction. *Notio* is considered a generic word and as such is divided into jurisdiction, as just explained, and *cognitio* or *notio simplex*. *Notio simplex* consists in the bare faculty of taking cognizance of a cause and judging a cause, the execution of which is left to the one with the power of jurisdiction.[21] Practically regarded, all the details of a trial come under the power called *notio*.[22] The concepts of jurisdiction and notion are made more clear when one considers the different procedural systems that were in use for the administration of justice.

Judicial matters were successively expedited according to three different systems. During the regal period of Roman history, it seems that the King was the sole judge, and if any procedural rules were followed they are lost in antiquity.[23] During the period of the republic, the system of *legis actio* prevailed. This system was founded on

editioni Graecam sanctionem . . . unaque Francisci Hotomani interpretationem latinam adnotationesque . . . ex Doctissimorum virorum Commentariis. . . . (Lugduni, 1557); Bartolus a Saxoferrato, *Omnia Opera* (6. ed., 11 vols., Venetiis, 1590), I, ad lib. 2 Digest., lex k, n. 3; Azo, *In Ius Civile Summa* (Lugduni, 1564), p. 49, nn. 1-3.

[18] Sanguinetti, p. 234.

[19] Perez, *Opera Omnia* (4 vols., Romae, 1827), I, p. 227.

[20] Donellus, IV, lib. XVII, cap. VI, n. XIV; Voet, Lib. II, Tit. I, nn. 42-43; Maroto, I, n. 573, in nota 1, p. 660.

[21] Voet, Lib. II, Tit. I, n. 2; Donellus, IV, lib. XVII, cap. VI, n. IX.

[22] Voet, *loc. cit.*

[23] Wenger, pp. 20-21.

oral recitations of certain sacred words based on statutes, by which the parties were given legitimate action in court.[24] The *legis actio,* as Cumin stated, were solemn forms of procedure, consisting of acts and words fixed with such rigid precision that the least mistake or alteration in them involved the loss of the suit.[25]

It must be remembered that the procedure *legis actio* was divided into the proceeding *in iure* and *in iudicio.* The first part was in the presence of the praetor, who exercised jurisdiction by arranging for the trial, establishing the claim under some *actio* and appointing a judge.[26] The cause was then handed over to the *iudex datus* and the procedure *in iudicio* began. In this system the judge only heard the cause and made the decision, which activity was called the power of *notio* or *cognitio;* his activity was not called *iurisdictio.*[27] Van de Kerckhove indicates that under this system the sentence of the judge was a mere private opinion, which was taken over and given force by the jurisdiction of the magistrate.[28]

Gradually the system of *legis actio* was so mitigated that about the time of the Empire (27 B.C.) it was succeeded by the formulary system. Under this system, while the twofold procedure remained, the magistrate was given greater freedom in the exercise of his jurisdiction and con-

[24] D. (1. 2) (2. 6). Cf. Wenger, p. 22; Van de Kerckhove, "De Notione Jurisdictionis in Jure Romano," *Jus Pontificium,* XVI (1936), 53.

[25] Cumin, p. 285.

[26] Van de Kerckhove, *loc. cit.;* Roberti, *De Processibus* (2 vols., Vol. I, ed. altera, Romae: Apud Custodiam Librariam Pontificii Instituti Utriusque Iuris, 1941; Vol. II, 1. ed., Romae, 1926), I, n. 45, 3 (hereafter cited Roberti); Roby, *Roman Private Law* (2 vols., Cambridge, 1902), II, 339 (hereafter cited Roby); Wenger, pp. 35, 94-132; Schulz, *Principles of Roman Law* (translated by Marguerite Wolff, Oxford: The Clarendon Press, 1936), p. 178.

[27] D. (42. 1) 5. Cf. Belloni, *Tractatus de Mandata Iurisdictione* (Parmae, 1625), pp. 14-20 (hereafter cited Belloni); Donellus, IV, lib. XVII, cap. 41; Van de Kerckhove, "De Notione Jurisdictionis in Jure Romano," *Jus Pontificum,* XVI (1936), 53.

[28] Van de Kerckhove, *loc. cit.*

trol over the entire procedure.[29] The main characteristics, as Cumin indicated, reflected a lack of precise detailed acts to be performed by the parties, and laid emphasis on the *formula* or written instructions appointing the judge, stating the extent of his power and defining the points of the case.[30] The judge, though still lacking jurisdiction, possessed whatever power the *formula* conferred, and, as Sohm (1841-1917) pointed out, he became an organ of magisterial power and was already beginning to assume the character of a subordinate official.[31]

An important and drastic advance was made during the reign of Diocletian in 294 by the introduction of the system of *cognitio extraordinaria.*[32] The outstanding change was that the magistrate or his delegate attended to the entire procedure, and there was no issue of a *formula.*[33] Under this system the magistrate and also the delegated judge exercised jurisdiction through the entire case.[34]

From all that has been said, it is clearly seen that the word *jurisdiction* pertained to judicial matters, and generally the use of the word seemed to be restricted in that way. Nevertheless, arguing from Roman Law texts,[35] Van de Kerckhove maintains that even in Justinian's time the word *jurisdiction* in Roman Law had come to be synonymous with power in the broad sense of the public power of ruling the community,[36] although Roman Law com-

[29] Sohm, p. 251; Buckland, *A Text-Book of Roman Law from Augustus to Justinian* (2. ed., Cambridge, 1932), p. 608 (hereafter cited Buckland).

[30] Cumin, p. 288; Van de Kerckhove, "De Notione Jurisdictionis in Jure Romano," *Jus Pontificum,* XVI (1936), 54.

[31] Sohm, p. 257; Belloni, pp. 14-20.

[32] Inst. (4. 15) 8. Cf. Van de Kerckhove, "De Notione Jurisdictionis in Jure Romano," *Jus Pontificium,* XVI (1936), 59-60.

[33] Buckland, pp. 603-604; Cumin, p. 285; Sohm, p. 290. See also Wenger, pp. 255-267, for an especially lucid presentation and comparison.

[34] C. (31. 1) 5; C. (3. 4) 1; C. (3. 3) 2. Cf. Belloni, pp. 20-23.

[35] N. (120. 6) 2; N. (5. 3); N. (11. un).

[36] Van de Kerckhove, "De Notione Jurisdictionis in Jure Romano," *Jus Pontificium,* XVI (1936), 60-65.

mentators of the middle ages restricted the word to mean judicial power.[37]

ARTICLE 2. NOTION OF JURISDICTION IN CANON LAW

The definition of jurisdiction as formulated by Roman Law commentators was taken over into the law of the Church and even quoted verbatim by such an eminent author as Panormitanus (1386-1453).[38] In examining the works of other early decretalists, it is apparent that the Roman Law definition of jurisdiction was accepted.[39] The word was used in designation of the public power of judging, although it was not expressly restricted to this meaning alone.[40] Certainly, that later canonical writers did not make such a limitation is most clear. Molina (1535-1600) and others expressly stated that the meaning of *ius dicere* is not restricted to the pronouncing of the sentence and the stating of what is equitable, but also contains the power to govern with laws and precepts and to administer justice.[41]

[37] Van de Kerckhove, *ibid.*, 64, in nota 1.

[38] Panormitanus (Nicholaus de Tudeschis), *Commentaria in Quinque Libros Decretalium* (5 vols. in 7, Venetiis, 1588), lib. I, tit. XXXI, c. X, n. 5 (hereafter cited Panormitanus).

[39] Cf. Sylvester Prierias, *Summa Sylvestrina* (ed. recens correcta, 2 vols., Venetiis, 1601), s. v. *de iurisdictione* (hereafter cited Prierias); Hostiensis (Henricus de Segusio), *Summa Aurea* (Venetiis, 1570), lib. I, tit. *de officio et potestate iudicis delegati*, in proem. (hereafter cited Hostiensis); Durandus, *Speculum Iuris* (4 vols. in 3, Venetiis, 1577), lib. I, partic. I, *de iudice delegato* (hereafter cited Durandus); Felinus Sandaeus, *Commentaria in Quinque Libros Decretalium* (5 vols. in 3, Venetiis, 1570), lib. I, tit. XXIX (hereafter cited Sandaeus).

[40] Van de Kerckhove indicates that a great deal of obscurity surrounded the word "jurisdiction" in early canonical usage. Cf. "De Notione Jurisdictionis apud Decretistas et Priores Decretalistas," *Jus Pontificium*, XVIII (1938), 10-14.

[41] Molina, *De Justitia et Jure, Opera Omnia Tractatibus Quinque* (ed. novissima, 5 vols. in 4, Coloniae Allobrogum, 1759), Tract. V, disp. II, n. 1 (hereafter cited Molina); Reiffenstuel, *Jus Canonicum Universum* (5 vols. in 7, Parisiis, 1864-1870), lib. I, tit. XXIX, nn. 2-3 (hereafter cited Reiffenstuel); Schmalzgrueber, *Jus Ecclesiasticum Universum* (5 vols. in 12, Romae, 1843-1845), XII, 146 (hereafter cited Schmalzgrueber).

Moreover, these later decretalists indicated that the definition of jurisdiction, as given by Roman Law commentators, was not fully applicable to Canon Law, because ecclesiastical power is not *de publico introducta,* that is, induced by the authority of the populace,[42] but is given to the Church by Christ Himself.[43] Nevertheless the name and canonical notion of jurisdiction found its historical precursor in Roman Law, and the concept was extended in such a manner that it embraced the notion of the entire public power of ruling in the Church.[44] Wernz (1842-1914) maintained that the word *jurisdiction* had this extensive meaning already at the time of Gregory the Great (590-604), although a more restricted usage had sometimes found its way into Decretal Law.[45]

Molina (1535-1600) adequately defined ecclesiastical jurisdiction as the *potestas publica circa regimen aliorum.*[46] This definition and the definitions of other canonists[47] have been crystalized in the Code of Canon Law by the use of the words *potestas regiminis.*[48]

[42] Reiffenstuel, lib. I, tit. XXIX, n. 2.

[43] Pius VI, const. *Auctorem fidei,* 28 aug. 1794, prop. 2, Synodi Pistorien. damn.—*Fontes,* n. 475. Cf. also Molina, Tract. V, disp. II, n. 5.

[44] Van de Kerckhove, "De Notione Jurisdictionis in Jure Romano," *Jus Pontificium,* XVI (1936), 64, in nota 2; Maroto, I, n. 573; Sanguinetti, p. 235; Crisci, *De Historia et Doctrina Delegationis a Iure in Iure Romano et Canonico,* Pontificium Institutum Utriusque Iuris Thesis ad Lauream, n. 3 (Romae: Apud Custodiam Librariam Pont. Inst. Utriusque Iuris, 1938), p. 13 (hereafter cited Crisci).

[45] Wernz, *Ius Decretalium* (6 vols., Vol. II, *Ius Constitutionis Ecclesiae Catholicae,* 3. ed., Prati, 1915; Vol. VI, *Ius Poenale Ecclesiae Catholicae,* 1. ed., Prati, 1913), II, n. 3, in nota 19 (hereafter cited Wernz).

[46] Molina, Tract. V, disp. II, n. 1.

[47] Sanguinetti, p. 235; Schmalzgrueber, XII, 146; Reiffenstuel, lib. I, tit. XXIX, nn. 3-6; D'Annibale, *Summula Theologiae Moralis* (3. ed., 3 vols., Romae, 1891-1892), I, n. 71 (hereafter cited D'Annibale).

[48] Canon 196.

CHAPTER II

DEFINITION OF DELEGATED POWER

In any society the power of constituted authority must be commensurate with the end to be obtained. With material growth and increased complexity of organization, the impossibility of constituted authority to attend personally to all affairs becomes evident. Therefore, delegation or acting through a substitute is the natural step.[1]

The basic notion of delegation can be found in two Rules of Law of Boniface VIII (1294-1303) which stated: *"Potest quis per alium, quod potest facere per seipsum;"* and *"Qui facit per alium, est perinde, ac si faciat per seipsum."*[2] These were based on the Rule of Law found in the civil law of Justinian which stated: *"Quod iussu alterius solvitur, pro eo est, quasi ipsi solutum esset."*[3] The idea here was the substitution and representation of one person for another.[4] This notion of delegation moreover was, as Kearney aptly states, "natural, not artificial; the most elementary reasoning suggests its accuracy. It is a proximate deduction of the very law of nature, and its first origin antedates the codification of all law."[5]

ARTICLE 1. DELEGATION ACCORDING TO ROMAN LAW

In Roman Law the words *delegatio, delegatus, delegare* fulfilled the generic notion of substitution and had a twofold usage. In the first place, "to delegate" was to give to a creditor another who would act in the place of the original debtor; secondly, a delegate was one who, representing the authority of the delegator but having no jurisdiction of his

[1] Wernz, II, n. 551.

[2] Reg. 68, 72, R. J., in VI°. Cf. Roelker, "An Introduction to the Rules of Law," *The Jurist* (Washington, D. C., 1941—), X (1950), 424.

[3] D. (50. 17) 180. Cf. Reiffenstuel, *Tract. de Reg. Juris in VI°*, Reg. LXVIII, n. 1; Reg. LXXII, n. 1.

[4] Reiffenstuel, *op. cit.*, Reg. LXVIII, nn. 1-2; Reg. LXXII, nn. 1-3.

[5] Kearney, p. 1.

own, was given some case in order that he might bring it to conclusion.[6] The first of these two is technically designated as *delegatio*; the other pertained to jurisdiction or judicial matters. These will be treated successively.

Section I. DELEGATIO *in the Technical Sense*

The generic notion of delegation was applied specifically and in a technical way in the legislation on obligations. Roman Law provided a means whereby one could extinguish one's own debt by transferring it into a new obligation for someone else.[7] This was accomplished by a kind of novation which was called *delegatio*.[8]

This *delegatio* was the substitution of a new debtor for an old one, or the giving to a creditor someone else who would satisfy the obligation.[9] Thus, suppose that James was in debt to John and at the same time Albert owed James an equal amount. By means of delegation James extinguished his debt to John by delegating it to Albert. For this transaction the consent of John was necessary, lest his rights be placed in jeopardy;[10] but, once his consent had been given, the debt of James became extinct, so that no further claim could be lodged against him even though the delegate had failed.[11] This was the strict meaning of delegation in Roman Law. Moreover this institute must have been in frequent use in Roman society, for the

[6] Prateius, *Lexicon Iuris Civilis et Canonici* (Francof. ad Moen., 1581), s. v. *delegare* (hereafter cited Prateius); Calvinus, *Magnum Lexicon Juridicum* (2 vols., Coloniae Allobrogum, 1759), s. v. *delegare* (hereafter cited Calvinus).

[7] D. (46. 2) 1 pr.; C. (8. 41); Gaius, III, 155—*Institutes of Gaius* (Part I, Text with Critical Notes and Translation by Francis de Zulueta, Oxford: At the Clarendon Press, 1946) (hereafter cited Gaius).

[8] Cf. Buckland, p. 570; Roby, II, p. 38; Cumin, pp. 267-279; Sohm, p. 386; Warnkoenig, *Institutiones Iuris Romani Privati* (4. ed., Bonn, 1860), nn. 1018-1023.

[9] D. (46. 2) 11—"Delegare est vice sua alium reum dare creditori. . ."

[10] D. (46. 2) 12; C. (8. 41) 1, 3.

[11] Gaius, III, 176; Inst. (3. 29) 3.

words *debtor* and *creditor* were of wide application, referring to persons who were in any manner obligated to another, not restricted merely to pecuniary transactions.[12]

In the present legislation of the Church this notion of delegation is no longer extant, although, as Kearney indicates,[13] its applicability in earlier ecclesiastical jurisprudence can be seen in a decision of the Rota.[14] The cessation of delegation in this technical sense is not expressly mentioned in Roman Law; however, since a contract was involved, at least two ways may be ascertained inferentially. Obviously, a satisfying of the debt pointed to one way. Mutual waiver pointed out another way, as was indicated in the rule of Roman Law, which stated that what is entered into by mutual consent can be dissolved by the same.[15]

Section II. Delegation in the Broad Sense

Besides the technical use of the word *delegation* in Roman Law, there was operative a generic concept particularly with reference to jurisdictional or judicial matters. In the execution of judicial matters Roman Law had divisions which form a parity with, and indeed formed the foundation for, what today is called ordinary and delegated jurisdiction in Canon Law.[16] But prior to any definition of these

[12] D. (50. 16) 108; D. (50. 16) 222; D. (50. 16) 11. See also Poste, *Gaii Institutiones or Institutes of Roman Law by Gaius* (Translation and Commentary, 4. ed., revised and enlarged by E. A. Whittuck, Oxford, 1904), pp. 381-382.

[13] Kearney, p. 10. The word *delegare* or its variations are used 133 times in the Code of Canon Law, but never does its meaning approach this Roman Law concept.—Cf. Lauer, *Index Verborum Codicis Juris Cononici* (Romae: Typis Polyglottis Vaticanis, 1941), s. v. *delegatio, etc.*

[14] *Sacrae Rotae Romanae Decisiones Nuperrimae,* collectio complectens decisiones ab anno MDCLXXXIV usque ad annum MDCCVI (9 vols. in 10, Romae, 1751-1763), Vol. 3, decis. CLXIX (28 jan. 1692), nn. 5-6 (hereafter cited *Nuperrimae*).

[15] D. (50. 17) 35.

[16] Crisci, p. 10; Maroto, I, n. 698, in nota 2, p. 825.

two species of jurisdiction, it is imperative to mention the admitted lack of precision among authors and the subsequent confusion that arose concerning delegated jurisdiction in Roman Law and its comparison to the canonical notion.[17]

A. Exposition of the Term

The division of jurisdiction which is pertinent to the present treatise is the one that was based upon the terminology *"suo iure"* and *"alieno beneficio."*[18] Some persons possessed jurisdiction *suo iure* or in their own right and by means of the office which they held in their own name. These were endowed with ordinary or proper jurisdiction and being thus officially constituted they could expedite judicial matters in their own name and authority.[19]

In distinction to this, Roman Law texts clearly spoke of jurisdiction that was transmitted to others who thus enjoyed power, not in their own name or by reason of a proper office, but merely from the mandate or commission of another.[20] Consequently the exercise of this power was always undertaken *alieno beneficio.* This power was called mandated jurisdiction, and substantially corresponded to the canonical notion of delegation *ab homine.*[21] Another kind of delegation was that which by law, or by decree of the senate (*senatusconsultum*), or by imperial constitution, was specially assigned (*specialiter tributa*) to some-

[17] Maroto, I, n. 698, in nota 2, C., p. 827; Donellus, IV, lib. XVII, cap. VI, n. XII, in nota 18; Voet, Lib. II, Tit. I, n. 7; Crisci, pp. 16-17 and p. 17, in nota 30.

[18] D. (2. 1) 5—". . . qui eam iurisdictionem suo iure, non alieno beneficio habet."

[19] Crisci, p. 16; Donellus, IV, lib. XVII, cap. VII, n. II; Voet, Lib. II, Tit. I, n. 6; Roberti, I, n. 140, I, 1.

[20] D. (1. 16) 4, 5, 12, 13; D. (1. 21) (1. 1); D. (2. 1) 5, 16; D. (4. 8) (32. 16); D. (34. 2) 1.

[21] Crisci, p. 17; Conrad, *Die iurisdictio delegata im römischen und kanonischen Recht,* Inaugural—Dissertation (Köln, 1930), § 12, p. 57 (hereafter cited Conrad); Maroto, I, n. 698, in nota 2, p. 826.

one.[22] Such a delegate was empowered not by reason of a magisterial office (*iure magistratus*) of his own, but from a special concession. This bore some likeness to the canonical notion of delegation *a iure*.[23]

Prior to the inception of the procedural system of *extraordinaria cognitio*, judges called *iudices dati*[24] were named to hear a specific case, but acted only with the "notional power." These were not considered delegates, since they heard the case in their own name.[25] Van de Kerckhove indicates that under the *legis actio* system the sentence of the judge was a mere private opinion which was taken over and given force by the magistrate. Under the *formula* system the sentence of the judge was no longer looked upon as a mere private opinion, but contained some juridic element.[26] However, their function was not looked upon as being jurisdictional, although gradually it assumed this aspect.[27]

Under the *extraordinaria cognitio* system some judges were constituted for a determined cause by one who had proper power, and these were called *iudices delegati*[28] and enjoyed true delegated jurisdiction.[29] Hence delegated jurisdiction was defined as that by which one acted in and with the power of another, having nothing properly his own.[30]

[22] D. (1. 21) 1; Gaius, I, 4-5.

[23] Maroto, *loc. cit.;* Crisci, pp. 18-19. However, it is readily admitted that there is a dispute among commentators concerning the historical basis in Roman Law for the notion of delegation *a iure* according to the Code.—Cf. Crisci, pp. 20-23; Roberti, I, n. 140, I; Conrad, § 4, p. 34; § 12, p. 59; Maroto, I, n. 704, in nota 1, f., pp. 841-842.

[24] Inst. (4. 17) *tot. tit.;* D. (1. 18) 5; D. (1. 14) 4; D. (42. 1).

[25] Belloni, p. 10.

[26] Van de Kerckhove, "De Notione Jurisdictionis in Jure Romano," *Jus Pontificium,* XVI (1936), 53-54.

[27] Sohm, p. 257; Belloni, pp. 14-20.

[28] C. (3. 1) 5, 6; C. (3. 3); C. (3. 4).

[29] Belloni, p. 393; Roberti, I, n. 140, I, 1.

[30] D. (2. 1) 16—"... delegatus ... fungetur vice eius qui mandavit,

B. The Cessation of Delegation

There is abundant legislation in Roman Law pertaining to the cessation of mandated or delegated jurisdiction. It is evident that when a delegated judge died, his power ceased.[31] Paulus (†c. 231) pointed out that besides physical death, civil death, such as *capitis minutio,* also brought an end to the power of a judge.[32] Also some permanent incapacitating effect, such as loss of reason, disqualified a judge from acting, and a new judge would be appointed.[33] The *Digest* does not state whether a delegated judge had the right of renunciation, although it seems to have denied this right to the *iudex datus,* who could be forced to judge a case.[34]

Because of the very nature of delegated power, it ceased by the death of the delegator, unless prior to that death the delegate had begun to use the power transferred.[35] Revocation of the delegation was also admitted, because certainly if one had the right to delegate another, that one had the right to withdraw such representation.[36]

Depending upon the conditions or restrictions attached by the delegator, such as delegation for a certain case or a certain person,[37] or for a predetermined time,[38] the power of the delegate ceased accordingly. Delegation also ceased upon the completion of the case.[39]

non sua." D. (1. 21) (1. 1)—"... delegatus proprium nihil habet." Cf. Donellus, IV, lib. XVII, cap. VIII, nn. I-III; Prateius, s. v. *delegare;* Voet, Lib. II, Tit. I, n. 1; Strykius, *Opera Omnia* (8 vols., Frankofurti et Lipsiae, 1743), V, Disp. I, Cap. I, n. 3; Calvinus, s. v. *delegatio.*

[31] D. (5. 1) 32; D. (5. 1) 60; D. (50. 4) (18. 14).

[32] D. (4. 5) (5. 2).

[33] D. (5. 1) 18. Cf. Belloni, p. 395.

[34] D. (5. 1) (49. 1); D. (5. 1) 30.

[35] D. (2. 1) 6; *Glossa* ad D. (2. 1) 6, s. v. *antequam;* Belloni, pp. 377-378; Donellus, IV, lib. XVII, cap. XXVI, n. VIII.

[36] D. (5. 1) 58; D. (1. 16) (6. 1). See also Belloni, pp. 389-391; Donellus, IV, lib. XVII, cap. XXVI, n. VI.

[37] D. (2. 1) (16. 17).

[38] D. (5. 1) 32; Inst. (4. 12) pr.

[39] D. (42. 1) 55.

ARTICLE 2. DELEGATION ACCORDING TO CANON LAW

Section I. Definitions

It has already been mentioned that Decretal Law made use of the Roman Law notion of jurisdiction. In a similar manner the terminology of Roman Law relative to delegated jurisdiction found its way into early Canon Law and helped to formulate what today is called ordinary and delegated jurisdiction.[40] The general principles surrounding the institute of delegation received their pre-Code excellence in the law of the Decretals, in which special titles were devoted to the office and power of delegated judges.[41] As these titles indicate, the law of the Decretals continued to restrict itself to the consideration of delegated judges, and, as Kearney says, the principles envisioning general delegated power were then not being elaborated.[42] It is also to be observed from these titles that the term *delegata iurisdictio* gradually superseded the Roman Law term *iurisdictio mandata.*[43]

Early decretalists such as Hostiensis († 1271),[44] Durandus (1237-1296),[45] and Panormitanus (1386-1453)[46] were

[40] Crisci, pp. 17-18; Van de Kerckhove, "De Notione Jurisdictionis in Jure Romano," *Jus Pontificium,* XVI (1936), 64, in nota 2; Maroto, I, n. 698, in nota 2, p. 825. For a detailed exposition of the similarity and decided differences between the Roman Law and Canon Law notions of delegated jurisdiction, cf. Maroto, I, pp. 825-830, 838-844.

[41] X, *de officio et potestate iudicis delegati,* I, 29; *eo. tit.,* I, 14, in VI°; *eo. tit.,* I, 8, in Clem.

[42] Kearney, pp. 35-36. However, Sandaeus (lib. I, tit. XXIX, nn. 2-3, in proem.) spoke of the general scope of Title 29 and did not limit it to jurisdiction.

[43] Maroto, I, n. 704, in nota 1, B, p. 839; Conrad, § 12, p. 57; Crisci, p. 17.

[44] "Is cui causa committitur terminanda vel exequenda vices delegantis representans, et in iurisdictione proprium nihil habens."—Hostiensis, lib. I, *de officio et potestate iudicis delegati,* n. 1.

[45] "Delegatus est is qui ex alterius commissione alicuius causae recipit iudicialem cognitionem."—Durandus, lib. I, partic. I, *de iudice delegato,* § 1.

[46] "... delegatus geret vices delegantis.... non habet iurisdictionem iure proprio, sed iure delegantis."—Panormitanus, lib. I, tit. XXIX, c. XI, n. 1.

content to use the Roman Law definition of delegated jurisdiction without attempting to distinguish it from the canonical notion, and perhaps rightly so, since in Canon Law delegated jurisdiction is substantially in harmony with the Roman Law notion of mandated or delegated jurisdiction.[47] Later canonical writers continued this practice.[48]

The Code of Canon Law has reproduced the underlying concept in all these definitions and presents a concise definition of delegated power. Delegated power is that which is committed to a person; and, by contrast, ordinary power is that which is annexed to an office by the law itself.[49] Hence by reason of the title or source or proximate cause from which it is derived, all jurisdiction is specifically divided into ordinary or delegated power, so that this division is natural and totally adequate; there is no middle term between the two.[50]

If there be pointed out the essential characteristics or notes of ordinary power, a clearer understanding of the nature of delegated power will be obtained. From the definition of ordinary power as found in the Code two essential notes appear, namely, that it be attached to an ecclesiastical office and that this annexation result from the law itself.[51] Kearney moreover conclusively maintains that this

[47] Maroto, I, n. 704, in nota 1, A, p. 839; Crisci, p. 17.

[48] Cf. Prierias, s. v. *delegatus*, n. 1; Reiffenstuel, lib. I, tit. XXIX, nn. 12, 27-42; Pirhing, *Jus Canonicum in V Libros Decretalium* (ed. novissima, 5 vols. in 4, Dilingae, 1722), lib. I, tit. XXIX, n. 1 (hereafter cited Pirhing); Wernz, II, n. 557; Molina, Tract. V, disp. XII, n. 2; Gonzalez-Tellez, *Commentaria Perpetua in Singulos Textus Quinque Librorum Decretalium Gregorii IX* (5 vols., Lugduni, 1623), lib. I, tit. XXIX, c. XI, n. 5 (hereafter cited Gonzalez-Tellez).

[49] Canon 197, § 1—"Potestas iurisdictionis ordinaria ea est quae ipso iure adnexa est officio; delegata, quae commissa est personae."

[50] Sanguinetti, pp. 236-237; Maroto, I, n. 688; Brys, *Juris Canonici Compendium* (2 vols., Vol. I, 10. ed. (post Codicem 2ª), Brugis: Desclée de Brouwer et Sii, 1947), I, n. 346, in nota 2 (hereafter cited Brys).

[51] Sanguinetti, pp. 241-242; Maroto, I, n. 699; Coronata, *Institutiones Iuris Canonici* (5 vols., Taurini-Romae: Marietti. Vol. I, 3. ed., 1947; Vol. III, ed. altera, 1941; Vol. IV, ed. altera, 1945), I, n. 278 (hereafter cited Coronata).

office is to be accepted in the strict sense of the word as found in the Code, and that the annexation of power is done antecedently to the bestowal of the office to a person, so that the power is identified with the office.[52]

Delegated power, therefore, is that which is directly and *per se* not antecedently annexed to an ecclesiastical office, and hence is conferred to a person by a commission or mandate which is done by the injunction of another or by disposition of law.[53] Consequently, it is the person of the delegate that constitutes the differentiating note between ordinary and delegated power.[54] Delegation is given, as Suarez (1548-1617) said, not through some internal consecration or physical faculty, but merely through a moral concession or deputation.[55] It should be pointed out that nowhere in the Code is it stated that this deputation or delegation must be given. It is a gratuitous concession,[56] and by its nature it lacks the note of perpetuity.[57]

[52] Kearney, pp. 54-55; Toso, *Ad Codicem Juris Canonici... Commentaria Minora* (2 Lib. in 5 Tom., Lib. I, *Normae Generales*, 2. ed., Taurini-Romae: Marietti, 1921; Lib. II, *De Personis*, Tom. I, Taurini-Romae: Marietti, 1922), Lib. II, Tom. I, p. 177 (hereafter cited Toso). Blat maintains that the annexation need not be to an office in the strict sense.—Cf. *Commentarium Textus Codicis Iuris Canonici*, Lib. II, *De Personis* (ed. altera, Romae, 1921), n. 146 (hereafter cited Blat, II).

[53] Sanguinetti, p. 242; Brys, I, n. 365; Coronata, I, n. 285.

[54] Kearney, p. 58; Maroto, I, n. 704, c.

[55] Suarez, *Opera Omnia* (ed. nova, 28 vols., Parisiis, 1856-1861), Vol. 22, disp. XXVI, sect. I, ad proem. (hereafter cited Suarez).

[56] Suarez, Vol. 22, disp. XXVI, sect. III, n. 1; Sanchez, *De Sancto Matrimonii Sacramento* (ed. posterior et accuratior, 3 vols. in 1, Venetiis, 1726), lib. III, disp. XXVI, n. 8 (hereafter cited Sanchez); Pichler, *Ius Canonicum secundum Quinque Decretalium Titulos Gregorii Papae IX explicatum* (2 vols., Ravennae, 1741), lib. I, tit. XXIX, n. 19 (hereafter cited Pichler); Brys, I, n. 285, 4°.

[57] Suarez, Vol. 22, disp. XXVI, sect. III, nn. 2-6. He pointed out one exception to this when he maintained that delegated power for hearing confessions of the faithful *in articulo mortis* is *ex se* perpetual.—cf. *ibid.*, sect. IV, n. 8.

Section II. Divisions of Delegated Power

Delegated power is subject to several divisions, as the Code indicates, though the later does not contain a detailed schema on this point. By reason of the agency delegating, delegation derives *a iure* when the law itself transmits power to a determined physical or moral person, but does not constitute such a person in an office in the strict sense of the word.[58] Delegation derives *ab homine* when power is given by way of a special commission to another by him who is empowered to act *per se* or *per alios*.[59]

A further division of delegation is the one that is founded on its extension. Delegation is universal when it extends to every species of power within the competence of the delegator, or at least totally to one determined class of affairs. Particular delegation is that which is conceded for a particular case or for several determined cases.[60]

By reason of the subject delegated, every delegation is personal in that it is always conceded to a person; however, even this admits of a division into personal and real delegation. Panormitanus (1386-1453) held that delegation was real when it contemplated the dignity or office possessed by the person delegated; it was personal when the person's proper name was used.[61] On the other hand, Gonzalez-Tellez (d. after 1673) defined real delegation as that which looked to the office or dignity enjoyed by the delegate, while personal delegation took cognizance of the

[58] Coronata, I, n. 287; Maroto, I, n. 705. It is disputed whether the Code contains instances of delegation *a iure*. The more common opinion seems to be the affirmative. For the contrary opinion cf. Roberti, I, n. 142.

[59] Canon 199, § 1. Cf. Brys, I, n. 365; Maroto, I, n. 705, A; Coronata, I, n. 287.

[60] Vermeersch-Creusen, *Epitome Iuris Canonici* (3 vols., Mechliniae-Romae: H. Dessain. Vol. I, 7. ed., 1949; Vol. II, 6. ed., 1940; Vol. III, 6. ed., 1946), I, n. 318 (hereafter cited Vermeersch-Creusen); Reiffenstuel, lib. I, tit. XXIX, n. 31; Maroto, I, n. 705, D; Brys, I, n. 365.

[61] Panormitanus, lib. I, tit. XXIX, c. XIV, n. 4.

personal qualifications (i.e. *industria personae*) of the delegate.[62] These definitions are still acceptable.[63]

An analysis of these definitions indicates that a further distinction relative to personal delegation is in order. Granted that every delegation will be either real or personal, it appears to be incorrect to say that every delegation looks either to the dignity or office of the person delegated, or to the personal qualifications of the delegate in the sense of an *industria personae.* In other words, a delegation may be personal in the sense of an *industria personae,* in which instance the delegate is selected to handle the matter on account of special personal ability, be it knowledge or prudence or influence.[64] On the other hand, a delegation may be personal, merely in opposition to a real delegation, in the sense that the delegate is selected because he possesses the ordinary ability required in any delegation. According to this latter meaning the concession of delegated power to this person is not motivated by the office or the dignity of this person, nor by any qualifications distinctly his own. The delegation comes to him simply as the consequence of an incidental concurrence in the elements of time, place, matter and person. The validity of this distinction appears to be conclusive from the wording of canons 57, § 2; 58; and 199, § 2.[65]

Section III. The Scope of Canon 207

From a speculative point of view it is of interest to determine the extension of canon 207. The interest arises mainly from this viewpoint because, for practical purposes, the end result of the application of canon 207 will be the same whether it is directly applied to all species of delegated

[62] Gonzalez-Tellez, lib. I, tit. XXIX, c. XIV, n. 8.

[63] Cf. Brys, I, n. 365; Kearney, p. 59; Maroto, I, n. 705, E.

[64] O'Neill, *Papal Rescripts of Favor,* The Catholic University of America Canon Law Studies, n. 57 (Washington, D. C.: The Catholic University of America, 1930), p. 182 (hereafter cited O'Neill).

[65] Cf. Kearney, pp. 83-85.

power or only indirectly by reason of the principle of analogy. Nevertheless the question may be asked whether canon 207 applies directly to jurisdiction alone, or to the power of orders and jurisdiction, or does it apply generally even to non-jurisdictional authority? This inquiry resolves itself into the more extensive question of the scope of Book II, Title V, in which this canon is found. That the principles of Title V do apply to species of power other than jurisdiction is beyond dispute.[66] The controversy enters with regard to the necessity of utilizing the principle of analogy of canon 20.[67]

The inscription of Book II, Title V, makes use of the most extensive terminology, namely, *De potestate ordinaria et delegata.* Because of this unrestricted heading, one may be led to conclude that within its scope is included not only the power of orders and the power of jurisdiction but all administrative and dominative power as well. It is correctly observed that the heading itself does not read *De iurisdictione ordinaria et delegata.* It is mainly on this ground that Title V is extended, by Maroto (1875-1937), to all kinds of power, so that for him there does not remain any need of eliciting the suppletory principle of canon 20.[68] If the legislator intended that Title V be restricted to jurisdictional matters, a mere change of word could have obviated the disputed question.

Despite the generic inscription of the Title, it is maintained by some that the canons of Title V refer only to the power of jurisdiction and the power of orders; any other types of power are governed by Title V only indirectly.[69] This opinion is based on the content of Title V, rather

[66] Kearney, p. 50; Coronata, I, p. 321, in nota 4; Vermeersch-Creusen, I, n. 311.

[67] Canon 20—"Si certa de re desit expressum praescriptum legis sive generalis sive particularis, norma sumenda est . . . a legibus latis in similibus; . . . ."

[68] Maroto, I, n. 694.

[69] Regatillo, *Institutiones Iuris Canonici* (2 vols., Santander: Sal

than on the rubric. Within this Title there is found explicit mention of both the power of jurisdiction and the power of orders. Since these two species of power receive explicit mention, the generic heading seems to be clearly determined. The Rule of Law, *Generi per speciem derogatur,*[70] could be cited for this opinion, inasmuch as the inscription to the Title seems to be modified by the very content of the Title.

Still another opinion limits the purview of this Title to jurisdiction alone, and thus calls upon the principles of canon 20 to provide the norms for all other kinds of power. Although not explaining or defending their doctrine Toso († 1946)[71] and Cocchi[72] hold this opinion. The present writer also prefers it. From the content of Title V it appears that the primary and direct object of the mind of the legislator is the power of jurisdiction and the principles governing it. This is admitted even by Maroto, although he maintained one of the other opinions.[73] Regatillo also says that the Title particularly refers to the power of jurisdiction.[74] Furthermore the inclusion of canon 210, in which the single mention of the power of orders is found, does not argue against this view.[75] In effect, as Kearney points out, this canon excludes more than it includes the power of orders.[76] Because of this practical exclusion and frequent

Terrae, 1941-1942), I, proem. ad n. 358 (hereafter cited Regatillo); Vermeersch-Creusen, I, n. 311; Oesterle, *Praelectiones Iuris Canonici,* Tom. I (Romae: In Collegio S. Anselmi, 1931), pp. 104-105.

[70] Reg. 34, R. J., in VI°.

[71] Toso, Lib. II, Tom. I, p. 164.

[72] Cocchi, *Commentarium in Codicem Iuris Canonici* (8 vols. in 5, Taurinorum Augustae: Marietti. Liber II, *De Personis,* Pars I, *De Clericis,* 4. ed. recognita, 1937; Liber IV, *De Processibus,* 3. ed. recognita, 1940), II, Pars I, p. 224 (hereafter cited Cocchi).

[73] Maroto, I, n. 694.

[74] Regatillo, I, n. 358, ad proem.

[75] Canon 210—"Potestas ordinis, a legitimo Superiore ecclesiastico sive adnexa officio sive commissa personae, nequit aliis demandari, nisi id expresse fuerit iure vel indulto concessum."

[76] Kearney, p. 49.

use of the word *jurisdiction*[77] the Rule of Law, *Generi per speciem derogatur,* seems better applied in this opinion than in the 'jurisdiction-order' opinion.

It may further be observed that since in Title V the primary and direct object of the mind of the legislator seems to be the power of jurisdiction, and since that legislator has already in canon 20 provided an adequate rule that governs any other analogous contingency, it is unnecessary to include under the scope of Title V any power other than the power of jurisdiction.

For these reasons it is concluded that Title V applies directly only to jurisdiction, and therefore canon 207 accordingly applies directly only to the cessation of the power of delegated jurisdiction; any other delegated power must reach its contact with the principles of Title V through the suppletory law of canon 20.

[77] Cf. canons 196; 197; 199, §§ 1, 2, 4; 200, § 1; 201, §§ 1, 3; 202, § 1; 205, § 1; 209.

PART TWO

THE CESSATION OF DELEGATED POWER

INTRODUCTORY NOTE

Having expounded the preliminary notions relative to delegated power, and thereby having laid the foundation for an understanding of what is to cease, one naturally looks to the main thesis of this work. If it be presupposed that the one who delegates is adequately empowered to do so, and that the person delegated is capable by nature and by law of receiving the grant of power and, moreover, that the delegation itself be rightly made, or more briefly, if it be assumed that the delegated power is actually possessed, the question now to be considered is this: how does delegated power cease, or what are the various ways in which the power of a delegate is extinguished?

It should be noted that throughout the present work the words *cessation, extinction, loss* are used in the sense of a total lack of the power delegated. This, therefore, concerns an inherent or absolute extinction of the power delegated, so that nothing remains and a new delegation is required if the former delegate is to be able to act. Certainly there is, in distinction to this, a loss of delegated power that could be called accidental or relative, as for example the suspension of delegated power that follows upon the incurring of certain censures.[1] The loss of delegated power of this latter kind is properly called a restriction or a suspension of jurisdiction,[2] since the delegated power actually remains *in habitu*, but is entirely dormant.[3] Upon the removal of the inhibiting circumstance, the subsequent warranted exercise of jurisdiction would not necessitate

[1] Canons 2264; 2284. Cf. *infra*, pp. 113-118.

[2] Brys, I, n. 375; Maroto, I, nn. 712, 716.

[3] Passerinus, *Commentaria in Sextum Librum Decretalium* (5 vols. in 2, Venetiis, 1698), lib. I, *de rescriptis*, c. V, n. 49 (hereafter cited Passerinus).

a new grant of power since the *ius radicale* had remained.[4]

It will be seen that sometimes the cessation of delegated power is caused by the will of the delegate or by the contrary will of the delegator, or sometimes by the fact that the delegation itself has been utilized in full. Generally, as is done by some authors, the cessation of delegated power may be divided *ratione delegationis, ratione delegantis* and *ratione delegati.*[5]

The Code of Canon Law itself does not directly use this division in Canon 207; it merely states in a succinct manner six different ways in which the extinction of delegated power is effected, namely: 1) when the mandate has been completed; 2) when the time for which the delegation was given has elapsed or the number of cases for which it was granted has been utilized; 3) when the final cause on account of which the delegation was made has ceased; 4) when the revocation by the delegator is made known directly to the delegate; 5) when the renunciation by the delegate is made known directly to the delegator and accepted by the latter; and 6) when the delegator loses his power, but in this instance the delegated power ceases only in two cases, namely, if in the delegation such a provision is made, or if the mandate of delegation contains a favor to be granted by the delegate to persons determined therein and the matter is still intact.[6] However, since this enumeration in the Code so easily lends itself to the aforementioned division, the present treatment will make use of it.

[4] Wernz, VI, n. 208. Here Wernz treated expressly of ordinary jurisdiction, but since power is actually transferred to a delegate, the term is applicable also under the present consideration.

[5] Maroto, I, nn. 713-715; Toso, Lib. II, Tom. I, p. 176; Kearney, p. 111; Coronata, I, n. 290.

[6] Canon 207, § 1—"Potestas delegata extinguitur, expleto mandato; elapso tempore aut exhausto numero casuum pro quo concessa fuit; cessante causa finali delegationis; revocatione delegantis delegato directe intimata aut renuntiatione delegati deleganti directe intimata et ab eodem acceptata; non autem resoluto iure delegantis, nisi in duobus casibus de quibus in can. 61."

In paragraph two of canon 207 the legislator has wisely made provision for the validity of acts of the internal forum which were inadvertently placed after the lapse of time for which the delegation was granted and also for like acts placed in excess of the number of cases committed.[7] Paragraph three of this canon refers specifically to collegiate delegation in so far as such delegation is extinguished in a manner peculiar to itself.[8]

CHAPTER III

CESSATION BY REASON OF THE DELEGATION ITSELF

The scope of this chapter is to examine the various ways in which delegated power is lost by reason of the delegation itself. It will embody three articles. Each concession of delegated power has a direct object, or that for which the power is given. This final cause may actually be fulfilled or, for some reason, it may simply cease to exist. The first case forms the subject-matter for the first article, the other case forms the basis for article three. The second article considers a grant of delegated power that is circumscribed to a definite time or for a determined number of cases.

It should be noted that in Title V, *De potestate ordinaria et delegata,* no special form is prescribed for the conferral of delegated power. Any form, whether in writing or verbally, will suffice so long as it clearly shows that the active subject really wills the concession of power to the *delegandus.*[9] Nevertheless, in so far as the delegate

[7] Canon 207, § 2—"Sed potestate pro foro interno concessa, actus per inadvertentiam positus, elapso tempore vel exhausto casuum numero, validus est."

[8] Canon 207, § 3—"Pluribus collegialiter delegatis, si unus deficiat, aliorum quoque delegatio exspirat, nisi aliud ex tenore delegationis constet."

[9] Brys, I, n. 370, II. Cf. also Suarez, Vol. 22, disp. XXVI, sect. I, n. 13; Laymann, *Theologia Moralis in Quinque Libros Distributa* (9. ed., Venetiis, 1630), Lib. V, tract. IV, cap. X, n. 15.

may be called upon to prove that he has been delegated, as a general rule it will be advantageous that the delegation be made in writing.[10] Indeed, canon 206 supposes that delegation was made in this manner. On the other hand, canon 879, § 1 expressly indicates that the concession of jurisdiction for the hearing of confessions may be given either in writing or verbally. Concerning delegation *in re iudiciali,* Roberti correctly holds that a written form is always required.[11] If delegation is made through a rescript, the rules governing the concession of rescripts need to be followed.[12]

ARTICLE 1. *Expleto Mandato*

Section I. Historical Note

It is stated in the Code that the delegated power is extinguished when the mandate has been fulfilled.[13] The historical antecedent of this legislation is found in a response of Pope Alexander III (1159-1181) to the Bishop of Brescia, in which the Pope declared that the authority or jurisdiction of a delegated judge ceased when he commanded the sentence to be executed or, if he was able to subdelegate, when he mandated this pronouncement to another, because in both instances[14] he had completely executed his charge.[15]

[10] Canon 200, § 2. Cf. Maroto, I, n. 709, 3ª.

[11] Canon 1642. Cf. Roberti, I, n. 141, IV.

[12] Roberti, *loc cit.;* Maroto, I, n. 709, 3ª.

[13] Canon 207, § 1—"Potestas delegata extinguitur, expleto mandato; . . . ."

[14] Panormitanus (lib. I, tit. XXIX, c. IX, n. 2) added the words "and the matter is no longer integral" on the part of the subdelegate. If the matter is still integral on the part of the subdelegate, the delegate's power was not irrevocably lost, since he could recall his grant. Cf. *infra,* pp. 72-74.

[15] C. 9, X, *de officio et potestate iudicis delegati,* I, 29; Jaffé, *Regesta Pontificum Romanorum ab condita Ecclesia ad annum post Christum natum MCXCVIII* (ed. 2. correctam et auctam auspiciis Gulielmi Wattenbach curaverunt S. Loewenfeld, F. Kaltenbrunner, P. Ewald, 2 vols., Lipsiae, 1885-1888), n. 14219 (hereafter cited Jaffé); *Nuperrimae,* Vol. 9, decis. CCXXVIII (17 martii 1706). Cf. also Gonzalez-Tellez, lib. I, tit. XXIX, c. IX, n. 3; Panormitanus, lib. I, tit. XXIX, c. IX, nn. 1-2.

Commenting on this response the old authors maintained that when the delegated judge, regardless of whether he had judged laudably or poorly, commanded the execution of the sentence, he was thereby voided of the power to retract the sentence and judge the case anew.[16] It was, therefore, as Reiffenstuel (1642-1703) stated, the completed execution of a definitive sentence, or, if that power was not granted, the pronouncement of the definitive sentence itself, that brought about the cessation of delegated power.[17] Moreover, this general rule was said to be applicable also to an interlocutory sentence,[18] in which the delegate as such declared that for some reason he did not have jurisdiction or was incompetent to expedite some matter.[19] Such a sentence, in this instance, had definitive force,[20] and hence the delegate was considered to have fulfilled his office.[21]

16 Barbosa, *Collectanea Doctorum tam Veterum quam Recentiorum in Jus Pontificium Universum* (6 vols., Lugduni, 1656), lib. I, tit. XXIX, c. IX, nn. 1, 3 (hereafter cited Barbosa); Leurenius, *Jus Canonicum Universum* (5 vols. in 3, Venetiis, 1729), lib. I, tit. XXIX, quest. DCCXXIII, n. 1 (hereafter cited Leurenius); Van Hove, *Commentarium Lovaniense in Codicem Iuris Canonici*, Vol. I, Tom IV, *De Rescriptis* (Mechliniae-Romae: H. Dessain, 1936), n. 272 (hereafter cited *De Rescr.*).

17 Reiffenstuel, lib. I, tit. XXIX, n. 147.

18 Cf. Lemieux, *The Sentence in Ecclesiastical Procedure*, The Catholic University of America Canon Law Studies, n. 87 (Washington, D. C.: The Catholic University of America, 1934), pp. 6-7 who explains this terminology.

19 C. 38, X, *de officio et potestate iudicis delegati*, I, 29; Potthast, *Regesta Pontificum Romanorum indo ab anno post Christum natum MCXCVIII ad annum MCCCIV* (2 vols., Berolini, 1874-1875), n. 9553 (hereafter cited Potthast). Cf. also Sandaeus, lib. I, tit. XXIX, c. XXXVIII, n. 1; Hostiensis, lib. I, *de officio et potestate iudicis delegati*, n. 11, in fine.

20 Panormitanus, lib. I, tit. XXIX, c. XXXVIII, n. 3; Fagnanus, *Commentaria in Quinque Libros Decretalium* (3 vols., Venetiis, 1709), lib. I, *de officio et potestate iudicis delegati*, c. XXXVIII, n. 6 (hereafter cited Fagnanus); Leurenius, lib. I, tit. XXIX, quest. DCCXXI; Reiffenstuel, lib. I, tit. XXIX, n. 130.

21 *Glossa Ordinaria* ad c. 38, X, *eo. tit.*, I, 29, s. v. *procedere non*

Notwithstanding the general rule, Van Hove (1872-1947)[22] and Michiels[23] indicate that limitations and exceptions were admitted among canonists. Thus, if a sentence was null because of the non-observance of the form of the mandate, the delegated power did not cease, since in this instance it seemed that the delegate did not fulfill his office or use his power.[24] The same applied to nullity that arose from an error of fact.[25] Contrarily, if the invalidity of the sentence arose from the non-observance of the law itself, the power of the delegate ceased, since his commission had been fulfilled, although badly.[26]

A second exception was founded in delegation *ad universitatem causarum* which, as Pirhing (1606-1679?) said,

debere.—Decretales D. Gregorii Papae IX, suae integritati una cum Glossis Restitutae (Romae, 1588); Fagnanus, lib. I, *eo. tit., c.* XXXVIII, n. 4; Reiffenstuel, lib. I, tit. XXIX, n. 130; Sebastianelli, *Praelectiones Juris Canonici, De Personis* (2. ed., Romae, 1905), pars 1, n. 126 (hereafter cited *De Personis*); Santi-Leitner, *Praelectiones Juris Canonici* (3. ed., 5 vols. in 4, Ratisbonae-Romae-Neo Eboraci-Cincinnati, 1903-1905), lib. I, tit. XXIX, n. 38 (hereafter cited Santi-Leitner); Bouix, *Tractatus de Judiciis Ecclesiasticis* (2 vols. in 1, Parisiis, 1854-1855), pars 1, p. 162 (hereafter cited Bouix).

[22] Van Hove, *De Rescr.*, n. 272.

[23] Michiels, *Normae Generales Juris Canonici* (ed. altera, 2 vols., Parisiis-Tournaci-Romae: Desclée et Socii, 1949), II, 464 (hereafter cited Michiels). Here he verbatim quotes Ojetti, *Commentarium in Codicem Iuris Canonici*, Lib. I, *Normae Generales* (Romae, 1927), p. 266.

[24] *Nuperrimae*, Vol. 3, decis. CCXXVI (21 apr. 1692), n. 1; Vol. 9, decis. CCXXVIII (17 martii 1706), n. 5; Pirhing, lib. I, tit. XXIX, n. 156; Gonzalez-Tellez, lib. I, tit. XXIX, c. IX, n. 3; Pichler, lib. I, tit. XXIX, n. 23; D'Annibale, I, n. 77, in nota 55; Huth, *Jus Canonicum ad Libros V Decretalium Gregorii IX* (Venetiis, 1843), lib. I, tit. XXIX, resp. 9, n. 4 (hereafter cited Huth). Van Hove (*De Rescr.*, n. 272, in nota 3) stated that this was the common teaching.

[25] Van Hove (*op. cit.*, n. 272) and Michiels (II, 464-465) admitted a dispute on this point.

[26] Pirhing, lib. I, tit. XXIX, n. 156; Van Hove, *De Rescr.*, n. 272; Pichler, lib. I, tit. XXIX, n. 23. Here Pichler (1670-1736) answered the objection that, since an invalid sentence has no effect, it cannot terminate the power of the delegate, by distinguishing *respectu partis* and *respectu delegati.*

was equivalent to ordinary power, and hence even after the sentence had been passed and executed, the delegate's power did not cease.[27]

A third exception was listed with respect to rescripts of favor. O'Neill (1900-1943) maintained that when the general rule, namely, the cessation of a completely utilized delegated power regardless of whether the work was done well or badly, was applied to rescripts of favor, it was interpreted as meaning that ordinarily the power of the executor ceased when the rescript was executed, even though it was executed invalidly.[28] Nevertheless Pirhing and others had earlier maintained that if because of error of law or of fact execution of a rescript of favor was invalid, the executor was able to repeat the commission.[29] This they argued from the fact that favors were to be interpreted broadly, so that some effect should accrue to the person to be favored.

It was admitted as the common opinion that an executor who proceeded extrajudicially was able to supply what was omitted in the execution for the reason simply that his power was not entirely defunct.[30] On January 15, 1894, the Sacred Penitentiary seemed to sanction this opinion when it issued a decision relative to an invalidly executed matrimonial dispensation.[31] A matrimonial dispensation was invalidly executed because, prior to the reception of the rescript, and hence apart from all recognition of its authenticity and integrity, the dispensation had been granted.[32] This response declared that the invalidly executed rescript could be re-executed without any further papal mandate.[33]

[27] Pirhing, lib. I, tit. XXIX, n. 156. Cf. also Pichler, lib. I, tit. XXIX, n. 22; Barbosa, lib. I, tit. XXIX, c. IX, n. 4; Wernz, II, n. 561.

[28] O'Neill, pp. 186-187.

[29] Pirhing, lib. I, tit. XXIX, n. 156; Pichler, lib. I, tit. XXIX, n. 22; Leurenius, lib. I, tit. XXIX, quest. DCCXXIII, n. 3.

[30] Van Hove, *De Rescr.*, n. 272, in nota 1, p. 254; Michiels, II, 465.

[31] *S. Poenit.*, 15 ian. 1894, ad II—*Collectanea Sacrae Congregationis de Propaganda Fide* (2 vols., Romae, 1907), n. 1858.

[32] Cf. O'Neill, p. 165, for pre-Code legislation on this point.

[33] O'Neill, p. 186; Van Hove, *De Rescr.*, n. 273, in nota 2.

This response, O'Neill said, has been extended and generalized by the Code of Canon Law, so as to include the possible re-execution of all invalidations and errors in the execution of rescripts.[34]

Section II. Canonical Commentary

The Code of Canon Law in a summary manner restates the earlier law by legislating that delegated power is extinguished when the mandate is fulfilled.[35] In the commentary on this canon some authors are content merely to rephrase the words of the Code and say that the delegate's power ceases when he completes the matter for which he was commissioned.[36]

A general statement of this nature leaves unsolved the problem of determining when the mandate is actually completed. To do this it should be noted that from the very nature of delegated power, since it depends upon the will of the delegator, that same delegator, as he sees fit, can circumscribe and limit the power conferred. This is clearly deducible from the law itself.[37] Therefore, the prime consideration in determining whether or not a mandate has been completed will be an examination of the terms set in the act of delegation. Let it be pointed out here and now, that the letter of delegation or the rescript or the oral expressions must be carefully noted. By reading this letter of delegation carefully and by taking cognizance of the extensions or limitations expressed in the act of delegation, one can effectively forestall many difficulties.

[34] O'Neill, p. 186.

[35] Canon 207, § 1—"Potestas delegata extinguitur, expleto mandato; . . . ."

[36] Beste, *Introductio in Codicem* (3. ed., Collegeville, Minn.: St. John's Abbey Press, 1946), p. 221 (hereafter cited Beste); Blat, II, p. 221; Toso, Lib. II, Tom. I, p. 177.

[37] Cf. canon 203. See also Kearney, pp. 105-106; De Meester, *Juris Canonici et Juris Canonici-Civilis Compendium* (3 vols. in 4, Vol. I, ed. nova, Brugis, 1921), I, n. 469 (hereafter cited De Meester).

Canon 207, § 1 itself does not determine when the mandate is actually completed, and consequently the solution to this question must be ascertained through a study of the canonical texts relative to the subject-matter delegated. Canon 201 suggests that the study be made in the canons that treat of judicial sentences, rescripts, privileges and dispensations, since it distinguishes judicial and voluntary jurisdiction. To determine the cessation of delegated power, the writer will follow the distinction *in causis iustitiae* or *in re iudiciali* and *in causis gratiae* or *in re voluntaria*, as the authors in the past have customarily done.[38]

A. *In Causis Gratiae*

As the word *gratia* indicates, there is under consideration here, from a negative approach, that grant of power that is not properly concerned with a judicial process.[39] In a positive sense, a *causa gratiae* or *potestas voluntaria seu non-iudicialis*, as it is called,[40] is that which is exercised without judicial form in a more or less administrative manner, as for example legislative power, or the power of dispensing and of granting favors.[41] One commissioned with power of this kind may be called a simple delegate, in distinction to a judge delegated to handle the *causa iustitiae*.[42]

In the cessation of the power of a simple delegate, there must be determined the basic question, namely, when is his mandate actually completed? Does completion occur when the bare essentials of the mandate are satisfied, or, again, what is to be said of an invalid execution of a man-

[38] Brys, I, n. 376, 1°; Maroto, I, n. 715, III.

[39] Kearney, p. 102; Maroto, I, n. 724, 2°.

[40] Canon 201, § 3. Cf. also canons 205, § 1; 1507, § 1.

[41] Regatillo, I, n. 358, 3; Ayrinhac, *General Legislation in The New Code of Canon Law* (London-New York-Toronto: Longmans, Green and Co., 1933), p. 359 (hereafter cited *General Legislation*); Vermeersch-Creusen, I, n. 316; Maroto, I, n. 724, 2°.

[42] Wernz-Vidal, *Ius Canonicum*, Tom. II, *De Personis* (ed. 3. a Philippo Aguirre recognita, Romae: Apud Aedes Universitatis Gregorianae, 1943), n. 368, II, c. (hereafter cited Wernz-Vidal, II).

date? The legislator has already answered these problems in canon 59, § 1, in which it is stated that, if an executor makes any mistake in the execution of rescripts, he has the right to repeat the execution.[43] Consideration should be given to the broad terminology of this canon. The word *executor* is used without any qualification, and thus it means not only the simple delegate but even one to whom the mere office of execution (necessary executor) is committed.[44] Moreover the expression *quoquo modo* is used, and thus it remains immaterial whether the error has intervened knowingly or unwittingly on the part of the executor.[45]

Because of the unrestricted scope of canon 59, § 1, it is commonly taught that in the exercise of voluntary jurisdiction the power of the delegate ceases only when the matter commissioned is validly executed.[46] Therefore, if in the exercise of the power delegated any invalidity occurs, whether it arises from a failure to observe the form of the mandate or to fulfill the essential conditions set in the act of delegation,[47] or whether the execution is undertaken before the reception of the letter of delegation or of the official information that the power has been granted,[48] the executor is not only permitted to repeat the execution, but is obliged to do so.[49] Even in the instance in which the simple delegate erroneously judges the re-

[43] Canon 59, § 1—"Exsecutori fas est, si quoquo modo in rescriptorum exsecutione erraverit, iterum eadem exsecutioni mandare."

[44] Cicognani, *Canon Law* (2. ed., authorized English version by O'Hara-Brennan, Westminster, Maryland: The Newman Press, 1949), p. 766 (hereafter cited Cicognani); O'Neill, p. 188; Michiels, II, 465. For an explanation of the term *executor*, cf. Van Hove, *De Rescr.*, nn. 254-255; Michiels, II, 448-452.

[45] Cicognani, p. 766; O'Neill, p. 188; Michiels, II, 466.

[46] Van Hove, *De Rescr.*, n. 273; Brys, I, n. 376, 1°.

[47] Canons 55 and 203.

[48] Canon 53.

[49] Cicognani, p. 766. Cicognani here seems to imply that even accidental errors could be corrected, whereas Michiels (II, 466) restricts the correction of an error to an essential matter.

script itself to be invalid because of subreption or obreption,[50] and thus refuses its execution, he is able to undertake the execution of the mandate when the true facts become known to him.[51]

The interpretation of those who set restrictions on the applicability of canon 59, § 1, and therefore regard the cessation of delegated power as having ensued, seems inadmissible. Thus Maroto, in correlating canon 207, §1 with canon 59, § 1, maintained that, although the potential re-execution of a rescript stands acknowledged, nevertheless when in reality the matter seems morally to be completed, the delegate cannot put his hand to the work again without a new mandate.[52] He gives no reason for this allegation which unwarrantedly restricts the effect of canon 59, § 1. Moreover his interpretation would place the whole question of the extinction of delegated power on the tenuous notion of a completed execution *moraliter loquendo.*[53]

De Meester also seems to invoke a restriction with reference to canon 59, § 1. He states that, if it is a question of a rescript containing the power of granting a favor to someone, the power ceases upon the first execution, whether it was done well or badly.[54] Granted that this was true under the earlier law, yet in canon 59, § 1, there is nothing to indicate that the word *executor* is meant to exclude a voluntary executor.[55]

Therefore *in re voluntaria* it can be concluded without hesitation that delegated power does not cease unless and until the mandate is validly executed. This view rests upon the unmodified terminology of canon 59, § 1, and also upon

[50] Canon 40.

[51] Van Hove, *De Rescr.*, n. 273; O'Neill, p. 188.

[52] Maroto, I, n. 715, III, in nota 3—"... cum negotium vere, moraliter loquendo, expletum censetur, delegatus sine nova delegatione, manus iterum ad negotium nequit apponere."

[53] Cf. Kearney, p. 112, and O'Neill, p. 188, who expressly reject this opinion of Maroto.

[54] De Meester, I, p. 203, in nota 4, and p. 320, in nota 2.

[55] Van Hove, *De Rescr.*, n. 273, in nota 2, p. 255; O'Neill, p. 188.

the common opinion as represented by the majority of canonists.[56]

B. *In Causis Iustitiae*

Now under consideration is that delegated power in the exercise of which a strict judicial form is used.[57] The concern at present, therefore, is to examine in greater detail the common statement that the jurisdiction of a delegated judge ceases when the definitive sentence has been issued.[58] As a general statement this conclusion is satisfactory, but it presupposes that the commission of the delegated judge is limited to merely pronouncing the sentence. This supposition is indicated by Brys and Bouuaert-Simenon when they say that the act of issuing a definitive sentence extinguishes the power of the delegated judge if he is not empowered to execute his sentence.[59] When the commission includes the power of execution, obviously that will be the determinant factor in the extinction of the delegated power.[60]

It has been seen that in voluntary jurisdiction the common and more tenable opinion maintains that delegated power is not extinct until the commission is validly fulfilled. Can the same be held when there is question of judicial jurisdiction? In other words, after giving the

[56] Michiels (II, 465, in nota 3) calls this opinion the *sententia communis.* Besides the authors already quoted in this article, cf. Ayrinhac, *General Legislation,* p. 366; Cocchi, Lib. II, Pars I, n. 224; Chelodi, *Ius Canonicum de Personis* (3. ed. curavit Pius Ciprotti, Trento: Libreria Moderna Editrice, 1942), n. 129 (hereafter cited Chelodi); Crnica, *Commentarium Theoretico-Practicum Codicis Iuris Canonici* (2 vol., Šibenik: Typis Typographiae Kačić, 1940-1941), I, p. 203 (hereafter cited Crnica); Coronata, I, n. 342; Bouuaert-Simenon, *Manuale Juris Canonici* (3 vols., Vol. I, 5. ed., Gandae et Leodii, 1939), I, n. 361 (hereafter cited Bouuaert-Simenon).

[57] Maroto, I, n. 724, 2°; Vermeersch-Creusen, I, n. 316.

[58] Regatillo, I, n. 367.

[59] Brys, I, n. 376, 1°; Bouuaert-Simenon, I, n. 361.

[60] Maroto, I, n. 715, III; Brys, I, n. 376, 1°; Cocchi, Lib. II, Pars I, n. 128; Ayrinhac, *General Legislation,* p. 366.

definitive sentence, may the delegate hear the complaint of nullity against the sentence and undertake the proper corrections?[61]

Admittedly the affirmative is not the more common opinion, for many hold, as in the earlier law,[62] that once the sentence is pronounced, whether it is given laudably or poorly, the power of the delegated judge is lost.[63] De Meester and Noval (1861-1938) rightly made exception for a judge delegated *ad universitatem causarum*, saying that the power of this type of delegated judge, since he has much the same stability as an ordinary judge, would not cease.[64] Wernz (1842-1914)-Vidal (1867-1938) seem to exclude even this exception.[65] Brys and De Meester, however, provide, and correctly so, for the reassumption of the commission when the invalid sentence results from the nonobservance of the form of the mandate, for in such a circumstance the judge has not used the jurisdiction, and hence it did not cease.[66]

Those who maintain that the delegated judge cannot receive the complaint of nullity against his sentence, rest

[61] Here an invalid, not an unjust sentence is considered. A sentence is valid when it is not affected with any of the defects listed in canons 1892 and 1894. Against the unjust sentence the remedy is an appeal; against the invalid sentence, the remedy is the complaint of nullity delineated in canons 1893 and 1895.—Cf. Kearney, p. 113; and also Coronata, III, n. 1394, d, who gives the definitions of this terminology.

[62] Schmalzgrueber, lib. I, tit. XXIX, n. 40; Reiffenstuel, lib. II, tit. XXVII, nn. 33-37; D'Annibale, I, n. 77, in nota 55.

[63] Cocchi, Lib. II, Pars I, p. 244; Brys, I, n. 376, 1°; Lega-Bartoccetti, *Commentarius in Iudicia Ecclesiastica* (3 vols., Romae: Anonima Libraria Cattolica Italiana, 1950), II, p. 1024, in nota 4 (hereafter cited Lega-Bartoccetti); Noval, *Commentarium Codicis Iuris Canonici*, Lib. IV, *De Processibus* (Augustae Taurinorum, 1920), n. 660 (hereafter cited Noval); Badii, *Institutiones Iuris Canonici* (2 vols., Vol. I, 3. ed., Florentiae, 1921), I, n. 148 (hereafter cited Badii).

[64] De Meester, I, p. 320; Noval, n. 660.

[65] Wernz-Vidal, *Ius Canonicum*, Tom. VI, *De Processibus* (ed. altera a Felice M. Cappello recognita, Romae: Apud Aedes Universitatis Gregorianae, 1949), n. 618 (hereafter cited Wernz-Vidal, VI).

[66] Canon 203, § 1. Cf. Brys, I, n. 376, 1°; De Meester, I, p. 320.

their opinion on the earlier law which stated that once the sentence is given the loss of power ensues.[67] Thus Noval typically argued that the continued existence of jurisdiction after the sentence has been given is to be predicated only of an ordinary judge or a universally delegated judge, since their power, being general, is not consumed through its particular use.[68]

In opposition to this opinion the following can be stated. It is argued by Roberti that the answer of Pope Alexander III, which is used as the basis for this opinion, does not in fact apply to the question proposed, but rather to the execution of the judicial sentence.[69] Moreover both Wernz-Vidal and Noval expressly stated that an invalid sentence is the same as no sentence at all, and hence it leaves the matter as it was before the sentence was given. Therefore, they said, an ordinary judge is able to proceed in the complaint of nullity.[70] However, they seem to be inconsistent when they then exclude a judge delegated for a particular case, since the same argumentation seems to apply.

The following arguments are advanced in favor of the opinion which holds that a delegated judge has not fulfilled his mandate by issuing an invalid sentence and, therefore, can reassume the process in order to bring it to a valid conclusion.

1) In canons 1893 and 1895, it is stated that the complaint of nullity is to be heard by the judge who gives the sentence (*coram iudice qui sententiam tulit*). It can be seen that no distinction is made between an ordinary judge and a judge with delegated power.[71]

[67] C. 9, X, *de officio et potestate iudicis delegati*, I, 29; Jaffé, n. 14219. Cf. Noval, n. 660; Wernz-Vidal, VI, n. 622, in nota 13; Muñiz, *Procedimientos Ecclesiásticos* (2. ed., 3 vols., Sevilla: Lib. de Sobrino de Izquierdo, 1926), III, 479 (hereafter cited Muñiz).

[68] Noval, n. 660.

[69] Roberti, II, n. 497, in nota 1, p. 232. Cf. *supra*, p. 26.

[70] Wernz-Vidal, VI, n. 622; Noval, n. 660.

[71] Roberti, II, n. 497; Kearney, p. 113, 1°; Vermeersch-Creusen, III, n. 242; Coyle, *Judicial Exceptions*, The Catholic University of

2) It is further observed that these canons do not state or imply that the delegated judge who pronounces an invalid sentence has fulfilled his office. The contrary is corroborated by analogy with canon 59, § 1, which instituted a change in matters of voluntary jurisdiction.[72]

3) From a practical point of view, since the complaint of nullity may be proposed immediately after the sentence, the matter, especially in the case of remediable nullity, could be expedited more easily by the delegated judge who actually gave the sentence.[73]

4) In canon 1878, § 1, the judge (*ipse iudex*) is permitted to correct material errors that have crept into his sentence. Of the authors consulted,[74] none exclude the delegated judge from this right, yet the *ipse iudex* of this canon is no more extensive than the *iudex qui sententiam tulit* of canons 1893 and 1895.[75]

5) Though one will readily admit the numerical superiority of the authors espousing the opposite opinion, nevertheless the opinion just proposed is also strengthened by extrinsic authority, for example, by Roberti[76] and Kearney.[77]

America Canon Law Studies, n. 193 (Washington, D. C.: The Catholic University of America Press, 1944), p. 63 (hereafter cited Coyle).

[72] Kearney, p. 113, 2°; Roberti, II, n. 497 and in nota 2; Coyle, p. 63. It appears that canon 59, § 1 directly refers only to voluntary jurisdiction, since rescripts of justice, according to Van Hove, are not given *in forma commissoria*.—Cf. *De Rescr.*, n. 273, *in fine*.

[73] Roberti, II, n. 497; Kearney, p. 113, 4°; Regatillo, II, n. 688.

[74] Lega-Bartoccetti, II, pp. 969-973; Roberti, II, nn. 463-465; Regatillo, II, n. 671; Coronata, III, n. 1406; Vermeersch-Creusen, III, n. 236; Van Hove, *De Rescr.*, n. 273; *et alii.*

[75] Kearney, p. 113, 3°.

[76] Roberti, II, n. 497.

[77] Kearney, pp. 112-114. For others who hold this view, cf. Kinane, "Jurisdiction in the New Code," *The Irish Ecclesiastical Record* (Dublin, 1864—), 5. series, XIII (1919), 216; Doheny, *Canonical Procedure in Matrimonial Cases, Formal Judicial Procedure* (Milwaukee: The Bruce Publishing Company, 1938), p. 346; Coyle, p. 63; Cocchi, Lib. IV, p. 380; Romani, *Institutiones Juris Canonici* (3 vols., Vol. I, *Jus Constitutionale*, Romae: Via Machiavelli, 1941), n. 324 (hereafter cited Romani, I); Regatillo, II, n. 688; Vermeersch-Creu-

On the basis, therefore, of these intrinsic and extrinsic arguments it is concluded that the invalid discharge of a judicial commission does not bring to naught one's delegated power, since, as even the opposition maintain,[78] to do something invalidly is equivalent to doing nothing.[79]

Another question may be raised. It has reference to the interpretation of a judicial sentence. It is stated in canon 1921, § 1, that the executor of a judicial sentence shall perform his office in accordance with the obvious sense of the decision. If a doubt arises, who is then competent to give an interpretation? On the basis of canon 1873, § 1, 1°, 2°, it may be stated that if the tenor of the sentence is such that it does not actually determine or define the controverted question, in the sense that the language used in the sentence is ambiguous, then it follows that the sentence is null, or as Schmidt aptly states, there is no sentence just as a doubtful law is no law.[80] In this instance, the delegated judge will proceed to correct his faulty sentence.[81] On the other hand, a mere subjective doubt concerning the meaning of the sentence may arise, or the decision may be unclear relative to its practical execution.[82] Can the delegated judge render an interpretation?

If the delegate is commissioned not only to give the sen-

sen, III, n. 242. Here Vermeersch-Creusen incorrectly cite Coronata, III, n. 1419, as holding this opinion. Coronata, *loc. cit.*, says outright that the delegated judge can receive the complaint of nullity against his interlocutory sentence, but denies this right with regard to the definitive sentence. However, he concedes that the reasons for the contrary opinion are certainly not to be spurned.—Cf. III, p. 338, in nota 8.

[78] Wernz-Vidal, VI, n. 622; Noval, n. 660.

[79] Kearney, p. 114.

[80] Schmidt, *The Principles of Authentic Interpretation in Canon 17 of the Code of Canon Law*, The Catholic University of America Canon Law Studies, n. 141 (Washington, D. C.: The Catholic University of America Press, 1941), p. 280 (hereafter cited Schmidt).

[81] Canon 1897, § 2.

[82] Schmidt, p. 280.

tence, but is empowered also to execute the sentence,[83] there can be no question about his power to interpret the sentence that he has given. The Code itself does not have an express provision on this question of interpretation, but as Schmidt, who wrote *ex professo* on the subject, points out, there is a constant juridic teaching affirming the power of a judge to interpret his sentence.[84] Schmidt does not restrict this right to the judge acting in virtue of ordinary power,[85] nor do the authors cited by him.[86] Confirmation of this right to interpret can be found in canon 200, § 1, which says that the concession of delegated power is understood to include those things that are necessary for the execution of that power.

Whether a delegated judge, if his commission does not include the power of execution, is able to interpret his sentence is problematic. This right to interpret is certainly sustained if express provision for interpreting the sentence is made in the act of delegation. The problem arises when no mention is made as to the right of interpreting the sentence. It could be argued that since the delegated judge can correct material errors that have crept into his sentence,[87] and since it is soundly probable that he can proceed to correct even the nullity (remediable) of his sentence, it would appear to be an undue restriction to hold that he cannot authentically interpret the sentence that he has given. This power seems to be part of his commission.

On the other hand, however, canon 200, § 1 clearly enacts a strict interpretation for particular delegation. And moreover, it is stated in canon 203, § 1, that whatever is done in excess of the terms of the mandate is invalid.

[83] Canon 1920, § 1.

[84] Cf. Schmidt, pp. 280-282, where abundant confirmation of this teaching is given.

[85] Schmidt, p. 282.

[86] Cf. e. g., Reiffenstuel, lib. I, tit. II, n. 362; *Glossa Ordinaria* ad c. I, X, *de postulatione praelatorum*, I, 5, s. v. *Interpretatus*.

[87] Canon 1873, § 1.

Wherefore, the better opinion seems to be this, that unless provision for interpreting the sentence is made in the act of delegation, this right does not belong to a delegated judge. The part of canon 200, § 1, which says that all power necessary to make delegated jurisdiction effective is also granted, does not stand in opposition to this view, since the delegated judge has effectively used his power when he has given a valid judicial sentence; the interpretation of that sentence pertains to its execution.

This same argumentation seems applicable even when considering the power of a delegated judge *ad universitatem causarum.* One might object by pointing out that according to canon 200, § 1, the power of such a judge receives a wide interpretation. This objection, however, is not to the point. Granted that a wide interpretation is given to the power of such a judge, nevertheless in no wise is it justifiable to read into a commission something that is not intended. The wide interpretation is applicable but only within the terms of the delegation. When the delegate is commissioned to give a valid judicial sentence, his power has been effectively used when the sentence has been given. Again it appears that interpretation of the sentence pertains to its execution.

ARTICLE 2. *Elapso Tempore et Exhausto Numero Casuum*

Section I. Historical Note

In canon 207, § 1 of the Code of Canon Law a second provision is made regarding the cessation of delegated power. This part of the canon legislates that delegated power is extinguished by the lapse of time or by the termination of the number of cases for which the concession was made. The historical precedents for the latter contingency have already been described above in the historical note to Art. 1, *Expleto Mandato.* The explanation there given applies to the present concept for upon a utilization of the number of cases for which the conceded delegation existed the mandate was regarded as having reached its completion.

The precursory legislation for the other, namely *Elapso Tempore,* is primarily discovered in a letter of Pope Alexander III (1159-1181) to one William, Bishop Elect of Chartres. In his response the Pope held that in cases which were to be decided within a certain time, the mandate ceased at the expiration of the time assigned.[88] This predetermined period of time began to run its course when the judge had received the letters of delegation.[89] If the term of expiration was set for a certain day, the power ceased accordingly.[90] However the earlier law provided for an extension of the period of time if the parties concerned gave their consent before the time had actually elapsed.[91] Of course, a prohibitory clause could rule out this prorogatory power of the parties.[92]

Section II. Canonical Commentary

Posited the fact that the power of the delegate depends on the will of the one who gives the commission, it is readily admitted that the grant of delegated power is subject to many variant hypotheses. Delegated power may be given conditionally or absolutely, for a determined time or without any such limitation, for one or several cases only or for all cases, and so forth.[93]

[88] C. 4, X, *de officio et potestate iudicis delegati,* I, 29; Jaffé, n. 11248. Cf. also c. 24, X, *eo. tit.,* I, 29; Potthast, n. 1423; *Nuperrimae,* Vol. 2, decis. CCCIII (17 iunii 1689), n. 2; Innocentius XIII, const. *Apostolici ministerii,* 23 maii 1723, n. 19—*Fontes,* n. 280; Benedictus XIV, const. *Apostolica indulta,* 5 aug. 1744, n. 3—*Fontes,* n. 344.

[89] C. 12, X, *de appellationibus, recusationibus et relationibus,* II, 28; Jaffé, n. 12293; *Glossa Ordinaria* ad c. 4, X, *de officio et potestate iudicis delegati,* I, 29, s. v. *certum terminus;* Panormitanus, lib. I, tit. XXIX, c. IV, n. 3; Pichler, lib. I, tit. XXIX, n. 21.

[90] Reiffenstuel, lib. I, tit. XXIX, n. 145.

[91] C. 4, X, *de officio et potestate iudicis delegati,* I, 29; Jaffé, n. 11248. Cf. also Panormitanus, lib. I, tit. XXIX, c. IV, n. 3; Reiffenstuel, lib. I, tit. XXIX, n. 146; Leurenius, lib. I, tit. XXIX, quest. DCCXXIV; Wernz, II, n. 561, IV.

[92] Sebastianelli, *De Personis,* pars 1, n. 126, e.

[93] Cf. Maroto, I, n. 574, d.

This present article is concerned only with the restriction by reason of time and by reason of the number of cases. It should be remembered that, whereas delegated power may not have expired in consequence of either of these two considerations it is possible that it has expired on account of some other reason. Consequently in this article, as in the other articles, the writer prescinds from all ways of extinction except the precise point under consideration.

Canon 207, § 1 merely states that when the time has elapsed or the number of cases has been terminated, the delegated power ceases.[94] This effect takes place automatically, so that no act of the delegator is necessary nor is any notification required.[95] However, in the second paragraph of this canon the legislator has benignly and prudently provided for the possibility of the delegate's inadvertent overstepping of the temporal or numerical limitation.

A. Lapse of Time

Delegation with a temporal restriction may be given in several ways. An express period of time may be established in the act of delegation. There may be delegated, for example, the power to dispense for six months, or to absolve for one year. Or the delegation may be given in such a way that the *terminus ad quem* is expressly mentioned, as for example when the power of absolving is granted until Easter Sunday. In the first instance, wherein the delegation is given for an express period of time, the computation is to be made according to the general norms for the reckoning of time as given in canon 34, § 3.[96] When the *terminus ad quem* is itself determined, no computation is necessary.

In canon 34, § 3 it is stated that if the time consists of one or several days and the starting point is explicitly or

[94] Canon 207, § 1— "Potestas delegata extinguitur ... elapso tempore et exhausto numero casuum pro quo concessa fuit; ... ."

[95] Brys, I, n. 376, 2°.

[96] Cocchi, Lib. II, Pars I, p. 245; Vermeersch-Creusen, I, n. 322; Maroto, I, n. 715, I.

implicitly set, then two possibilities occur. If the starting point coincides with the beginning of the day, the first day is counted. This may be illustrated thus. A delegate is empowered by letter to grant dispensations for six months beginning on June 10th. This first day is counted, and the delegate's power ceases at midnight on December 9th/10th. If the starting point does not coincide with the beginning of the day, that day (on which the power is actually granted) is not counted, and the computation begins only at midnight of that day. Thus, suppose that during the 10th day of June the bishop tells a pastor of his diocese that he is delegated to dispense for six months. Since the time does not coincide with the beginning of the day, the delegated power ceases at midnight on December 10th/11th.

Relative to the method of computing the duration of delegated power, it is of urgent importance that the act of delegation clearly contain mention of the inception of the *terminus a quo*. Without this designation, confusion may easily arise as to whether the computation is to be made from the beginning or the end of the day on which delegation is made.

While the computation of time is generally made according to canon 34, § 3, it is possible that delegation be granted without an explicit or implicit determining of the day on which the period of time is to begin. In this event the calculation of the duration of delegated power would be reckoned from a given moment on the day to the same given moment on another day.[97]

Although no distinction is made in canon 207, § 1, it is generally admitted that this rule, *"elapso tempore,"* does not apply to those matters that are no longer integral when the period of time expires.[98] Generally a matter of judicial jurisdiction seems to be no longer integral or untouched when the citation has been given; in matters of voluntary

[97] Canon 34, § 2.

[98] Coronata, I, n. 290, 1°; Maroto, I, n. 715, I; Regatillo, *Ius Sacramentarium* (2. ed., Santander: Administracion de Sal Terrae, 1949), n. 437, b. (hereafter cited *Ius Sacram.*).

jurisdiction, when the investigation to see if true reasons were alleged is begun; in matters of sacramental confession, when the confession is heard even though absolution is delayed.[99]

In the pre-Code law, as has been seen, express provision was made for the extension (prorogation) of delegated power beyond the time limit set by the delegator. The question arises whether this provision is enacted in the Code. The circumstances envisioned in this question must be understood.

Prorogation here does not refer to instances in which one has begun to use the power that has been delegated. This should be clear, for there is an express extension of power by the law itself in judicial matters that are no longer integral. Hence an extension by the judge with the consent of the parties is unnecessary. The legislator himself provides that the jurisdiction of synodal and pro-synodal judges does not cease at the end of the period of time for which they were elected or appointed, in so far as the law empowers them to bring to conclusion whatever matters they have begun to handle.[100]

This extension of judicial jurisdiction is generally applied also to the exercise of voluntary jurisdiction; *a fortiori,* to delegated judicial power,[101] for the reason that delegated jurisdiction becomes firmly founded in the delegate only when he begins to use the power conferred.[102] Hence the

[99] Coronata, I, n. 290, 1°. This question of the *res non amplius integra* will be further discussed at the end of Chapter IV.—cf. *infra* pp. 84-85.

[100] Canon 387, § 1—"... [iudices synodales vel pro-synodales—canon 1574, § 2] possunt tamen negotium iam coeptum ad exitum perducere...." The writer holds with Roberti (I, n. 106, II) that these judges are endowed with ordinary power, and thus the application of the principle enunciated in canon 1574, § 2 (which harkens back to canon 387, § 1) derives by way of analogy.

[101] Coronata, I, n. 290, 1°; Maroto, I, n. 715, I, 2°; Regatillo, I, n. 367.

[102] Canon 1725, 3°. Cf. Maroto, I, n. 715a; Lega-Bartoccetti, I, p. 203, in nota 1.

question being discussed here is this. May delegated jurisdiction be extended beyond the predetermined time by the delegate or the party or parties benefiting from the concession of power in cases in which the matter still remains integral? The very tenor of canon 207, § 1, and the considerations of the authors in respect to the provisions of this canon, seem indirectly to reject such a prorogation unless express provision for it were made in the act of delegation.[103] Then the extension exists actually by the will of the delegator.

Despite the words of the canon and the almost unanimous silence among authors on the direct question of prorogation, several were found to maintain an exception to the extinction of delegated power by reason of the lapse of time. Basing their remarks on canon 1634, § 2,[104] Brys[105] and Cocchi[106] state that delegated jurisdiction does not expire if, by the consent of the parties, the judge prorogues it before the predetermined time has actually expired. Lega-Bartoccetti maintain that delegated jurisdiction does not cease by the lapse of the aforementioned time when the parties in whose favor the time was predetermined desire that the mandate be fulfilled over a longer period of time.[107]

[103] Cf. Coronata, I, n. 290, 1°; Beste, p. 221; Cappello, *Summa Iuris Canonici* (3 vols., Romae: Apud Aedes Universitatis Gregorianae. Vols. I-II, 4. ed., 1945; Vol. III, ed. altera, 1940), I, n. 258 (hereafter cited *Summa*); Vermeersch-Creusen, I, n. 322, 2°; Regatillo, *Ius Sacram.*, n. 437, b-c; Chelodi, n. 129; Ayrinhac, *General Legislation*, p. 367; *et alii.*

[104] Canon 1634, § 2—"Termini autem iudiciales . . . , ante eorum lapsum, poterunt, iusta intercedente causa, a iudice, auditis vel petentibus partibus, prorogari."

[105] Brys, I, n. 376, 2°—"Excipitur tamen si terminus judicialis statutus, ante elapsum tempus, de communi partium consensu, a judice fuerit prorogatus (c. 1634, § 2)."

[106] Cocchi, Lib. II, Pars I, p. 245—". . . quoad tempus excipitur casus pro causis iudicialibus quo 'dies praefixus antequam transactus sit, de communi consensu partium prorogetur (c. 1634, § 2)'."

[107] Lega-Bartoccetti, I, p. 203—"Nempe cessat eius [judicis delegati]; . . . 4) Lapsu temporis praefixi in mandato, nisi partes, in qua-

It is not made clear whether these authors have in mind a matter that is still integral (*res adhuc integra*). It may well be that they contemplate otherwise (i.e. *res non amplius integra*) because, of the authors consulted, they alone made no mention of the prorogation that is accomplished by reason of the fact that the delegate has begun to use his jurisdiction. Such an extension of delegated jurisdiction is not an exception, since analogously the law itself grants to the delegate the power to complete the matter in hand.

If in their statements the reference is to a matter that is still integral, there seems to be a tampering with the express will of the delegator which renders that will ineffective. Certainly the delegate enjoys only those powers that are conferred upon him in the act of delegation, so that if he exceeds its limit he does nothing.[108] Moreover, when the will of the delegator expressly establishes a predetermined period of time within which the delegate enjoys jurisdiction, such provision is tantamount to establishing an essential condition which must be followed under pain of invalidity.[109]

Further, it is not out of place to question whether the Title, *De dilationum terminis et fatalibus,* in the Code[110] is even applicable to the present question. That the concession of delegated jurisdiction for a certain period of time should be considered a *terminus iudicialis* of canon 1634, § 2, seems doubtful for two reasons. The pertinent canons themselves seem to refer to delays that occur in

rum utilitatem tempus determinatum fuerat, patiantur ipsum mandatum expleri in longius tempus. . . ."

[108] Canon 203, § 1—"Delegatus qui sive circa res sive circa personas mandati sui fines excedit, nihil agit." The wording here does not expressly mention the element of time, but at least indirectly it seems included. Of course it is supposed that there is actually given a sufficient period of time, according to the judgment of the delegator, within which the delegation for a particular case can be fulfilled. This follows from canon 200, § 1.

[109] Canons 203, § 2; 55; 39.

[110] Lib. IV, Tit. III, Caput III.

the very exercise of jurisdiction in a judicial process.[111] This is indicated by the examples found in the Code.[112] Note also that if the delay occurred in the very exercise of jurisdiction, in the supposition that the aforedetermined time has elapsed, the jurisdiction is extended not by reason of a *dilatio iudicialis* but by reason of the fact that the delegate has begun to use his jurisdiction.

The second reason for questioning the applicability of the *terminus iudicialis* to the delegated jurisdiction itself is the explanations given by the authors. Except for the three aforementioned authors (Brys, Cocchi and Lega-Bartoccetti) none even allude to the alleged relationship between the prorogation of delegated power and the prorogation of a *terminus iudicialis*.[113]

It may be stated, therefore, that delegated power is extinguished by the lapse of time for which it was granted. Provision is made for the prorogation of power relative to those matters that are no longer integral, or that have been undertaken before the actual lapse of the time. If the matter has not been begun and no provision is made in the act of delegation for an extension of the time allotted, the delegated power automatically expires.[114] Obviously, if no temporal restriction is mentioned, the delegated power will endure until its cessation is effected in some other way.

Delegated jurisdiction, however, may be prorogued or extended by the grantor. For example, jurisdiction has been granted to hear confessions for five years. Before his time has elapsed the delegate receives notification that his power has been extended for another five years. The computation

[111] Cf. Canons 1634, §§ 1, 2, 3; 1635.

[112] See, e. g., canons 1715, §1; 1729, § 1; 1731, 2°; 1788; 1799, § 2; 1862; 1865, § 1. These are cited by Coronata, III, n. 1157, in nota 5, p. 67.

[113] Cf. e. g., Coronata, III, nn. 1157-1158; Regatillo, II, nn. 413-415; Wernz-Vidal, VI, nn. 181-188; Roberti, I, nn. 160-165; Vermeersch-Creusen, III, n. 70; and even Cocchi, Lib. IV, nn. 50-52.

[114] Roberti, I, n. 141, V.

of the second period of time is to be made, not from the moment that the prorogation was granted, but rather from the termination of the former grant.[115] If the time had actually elapsed, the computation of the new period of time would depend on the wording of the subsequent concession. If the words clearly indicate that the subsequent concession is merely an extension of the former grant, the computation would be made as stated above. If it appears to be a new grant, the computation will be made independently of the expiratory term of the former concession.

Concerning the subdelegation of delegated power the following observations are offered. According to the general principles of delegation, a delegate whose commission is restricted to a determined period of time is not able to subdelegate (if subdelegation is permitted) his power for a term that would extend beyond the *terminus ad quem* of his own delegation. Thus a local ordinary, in subdelegating his Quinquennial Faculties, is restricted to that period of time for which they were granted to him. Even a habitual subdelegated faculty is extinguished by the lapse of time predetermined in the Faculties from the Holy See.[116]

B. Number of Cases

It is entirely within the competence of the grantor to commit power to another with a restriction relative to the number of cases. The law states that, when there has been utilized the number of cases for which the delegation was conceded, the delegated power ceases.[117] Thus, by way of example, if a confessor has been given the power to absolve from five reserved cases, when this number of cases

[115] Regatillo, *Ius Sacram.*, n. 437, c.

[116] Eagleton, *The Diocesan Quinquennial Faculties, Formula IV,* The Catholic University of America Canon Law Studies, n. 248 (Washington, D. C.: The Catholic University of America Press, 1948), p. 45 (hereafter cited Eagleton).

[117] Canon 207, § 1—"Potestas delegata extinguitur . . . exhausto numero casuum pro quo concessa fuit; . . . ."

has been retired, his power *ipso facto,* without any intervention of the superior, expires.[118] The termination of the total number of cases that effects the cessation of the power presupposes that each of the cases has been brought to conclusion. This topic is directly related to the article *Expleto Mandato.*[119] Certainly the delegate has not used up his power until the mandate, which here includes each delegated case, is validly completed. It is obvious, therefore, that the clàuse *exhausto numero casuum* means not only that there has been used up the number of cases delegated, but also that each of the cases delegated has been brought to a valid conclusion.[120]

It should be noted also that just as there is no prorogation or extension of a temporal restriction at the hand of the delegate, so also there is no legal basis for extending the possession and use of a delegated power to a number greater than the number designated in the act of delegation.[121] The delegator is able to make provision in the act of delegation for such an extension, but such an extensible provision, which in no wise is to be presumed, would be dependent upon some future contingency.

Even subsequent to the delegation, the delegator is able to send notice of an extension of the number of cases. It should be noted that cases inadvertently undertaken in the internal forum in excess of the number of cases delegated are undertaken validly, and may be validly completed in virtue of canon 207, § 2. Moreover, when an extension of the number is received from the delegator, such cases undertaken inadvertently in the internal forum are

[118] Brys, I, n. 376, 2°.

[119] Toso, Lib. II, Tom. I, p. 177.

[120] Kearney, p. 114, c.

[121] Kinane indicated that prior to the Code there was a regulation to the effect that, if timely application for a renewal of faculties had been made, the prior faculties could be exercised in excess of the temporal or numerical limitation, even though the renewal had not been given. Such a regulation is no longer in force. Cf. "Jurisdiction in the New Code," *The Irish Ecclesiastical Record,* 5. series, XIII (1919), 216.

not to be subtracted from the number of cases designated in the subsequent extension.[122]

The subdelegation, when it is allowed, of power delegated with a numerical limitation obviously cannot be made for a number greater than the number of the cases originally delegated. Furthermore, the delegate would have to take into account the number of cases that he had already validly completed. It is impossible for him to validly subdelegate more than he actually possesses.[123]

C. Exceptional Provision For Acts Placed Inadvertently

Since the headings "*Expleto Mandato*" and "*Exhausto Numero Casuum*" are interrelated, one may question why the legislator has expressly provided for the latter. The fact that the Code includes both indicates the existence of a reason. This is emphasized when one notes that the *Schema* to the Code made no mention of "*Exhausto Numero Casuum.*"[124] It is further observed that the *Schema* did not refer to the favorable enactment that is now embodied in canon 207, § 2.[125] It may well be that specific mention was made of "*Exhausto Numero Casuum*" so as to more clearly set off the notable exception of paragraph 2. This paragraph orders that power granted for the internal

[122] Cf. Regatillo, *Ius Sacram.*, n. 437, c; Vermeersch-Creusen, I, n. 322, 2°.

[123] Reg. 79, R. J., in VI°.

[124] *Schema Codicis Iuris Canonici Sanctissimi Domini Nostri Pii PP. X*, cum notis Petri Card. Gasparri (Romae, 1912), Lib. II, c. 111, § 1 (hereafter cited *Schema C.I.C.*).

[125] Earlier enactments were even more restrictive in that no mention was made of inadvertence even with regard to confessional faculties.—Cf., e. g., Innocent XIII, const. *Apostolici ministerii*, 23 maii 1723, § 19—*Fontes*, n. 280; Benedictus XIII, const. *In supremo*, 23 sept. 1724, §§ 16, 28—*Fontes*, n. 283; Benedictus XIV, const. *Apostolica indulta*, 5 aug. 1744, § 3—*Fontes*, n. 344; ep. encycl. *Apostolicum ministerium*, 30 maii 1753, § 9—*Fontes*, n. 425. See Augustine, *A Commentary on the New Code of Canon Law* (8 vols. Vol. II, *Clergy and Hierarchy*, 3. ed., St. Louis, Mo.-London, 1919), II, 188, in nota 51 (hereafter cited Augustine, II).

forum is still validly used if through inadvertence the priest has not noticed that the time for which the delegation was given has elapsed or that the total number of cases has been utilized.[126]

The legislator has made this enactment in order to forestall the harm to individuals that is likely to ensue from a natural human defect in the Church's ministers. No sources are cited in the Code for this new legislation, as Kearney calls it.[127] However, such a precautionary clause was generally inserted in the confessional faculties from the Sacred Penitentiary.[128]

In examining the terminology of this paragraph, one will note that there is a decided difference between it and the supplied jurisdiction of canon 209. As Toso († 1946) deftly stated, it is one thing to prorogue jurisdiction, another to supply it. Jurisdiction that exists may be prorogued; that which does not exist may be supplied.[129]

This jurisdictional extension by law refers then to power that is granted for the internal forum (*pro foro interno*). This forum primarily and directly has regard for the spiritual benefit of the individual members of the Church; only secondarily and as a consequence does it redound to the public and common good of this society. This forum directly envisions a person's relationship to God, and only indirectly his relationship to the Church.[130] The exercise of jurisdiction in the internal forum may occur within the sacrament of penance or outside of confession. Since the law in no wise distinguishes, it is concluded that the enactment of paragraph 2 is applicable to either the sacramental or the non-sacramental internal forum.[131]

[126] Canon 207, § 2—"Sed potestate pro foro interno concessa, actus per inadvertentiam positus, elapso tempore vel exhausto casuum numero, validus est."

[127] Kearney, p. 117.

[128] Blat, II, n. 156; Brys, I, n. 376, 2°; Bouuaert-Simenon, I, n. 361.

[129] Toso, Lib. II, Tom. I, p. 179.

[130] Maroto, I, n. 718.

[131] Blat, II, n. 156; Kearney, p. 118; Vromant, *Ius Missionariorum*

Moreover, it is important to note that paragraph 2 does not state that the concession of delegated power be made exclusively for the internal forum, but only that when delegation is *de facto* granted for that forum, the power remains operative in the instance of inadvertence. Because of this it is proper to recall the general principles regarding the forum in which delegated power is to be exercised.

Delegation granted for the external forum may be exercised also in the internal forum, while that granted for the internal forum cannot be exercised in the external forum. Delegation granted for the internal forum may be exercised sacramentally or extra-sacramentally, unless the sacramental forum is expressly prescribed. Delegation granted without mention of the forum is presumed to be conceded for both the internal and external forum, unless the nature of the matter postulates otherwise.[132]

While paragraph 2 of canon 207 may in no wise be extended to the exercise of power in the external forum, nevertheless nothing prevents a provision and effect like that which is delineated in canon 207, § 2, from being enacted for the external forum by the delegator himself. The delegator could insert in the act of delegation a clause which would provide for the validity of acts inadvertently placed in the external forum beyond the temporal or numerical limitation.[133]

Besides the limitation which it sets for the exercise of power in the internal forum, canon 207, § 2 requires that a second condition be verified before the acts are considered valid, viz., the act must be placed while the subject exercising it is unmindful of the completed lapse of time or the terminated number of cases.

Inadventence in this paragraph is the lack of the mind's attention to the fact that the time has expired or the

—*Facultates Apostolicae quas Sacra Congregatio de Propaganda Fide delegare solet Ordinariis Missionum* (ed. 3. emendata, Paris: Desclée De Brouwer, 1947), n. 29 (hereafter cited Vromant); Romani, n. 324.

[132] Canon 202, §§ 1, 2, 3.

[133] Vromant, n. 30.

number of cases has been retired. Ignorance on the other hand would be a lack of due knowledge concerning the expiration of the time or the number of cases. Inadvertence here supposes that one has knowledge concerning the status of his power, but that in the very exercise of the power one does not advert to or apply his knowledge. This inadvertence must occur in good faith and hence must be actual on the part of the delegate.[134] Moreover, for the verification of the concept of inadvertence, it is difficult to see that the inadvertence could be of a character otherwise than that. In other words, it is impossible, when placing the act, to close one's eyes to the status of one's power and still consider it as inadvertence. Inadvertence supposes that the lack of awareness occurs when the act is placed; indeed, it is called forgetfulness or an oversight.[135] Furthermore, the law does not distinguish, and therefore, so long as the delegate by oversight or forgetfulness places an act in the internal forum, that act is valid, even though perhaps the inadvertence is gravely culpable in its source.[136]

It should also be pointed out that the law speaks only of inadvertence on the part of the delegate placing the act in the internal forum in excess of the temporal or numerical limitation.[137] Consequently the one benefiting from this act placed by the delegate may be fully aware of the status of the delegate's power; nevertheless, the act is valid as far as the delegate is concerned.[138]

The law speaks in the singular of an *act* placed through

[134] Coronata, I, n. 290, 1°; Naz, *Traité de Droit Canonique* (4 vols., Paris: Letouzey et Ané, Éditeurs, 1948-1949), I, n. 494, *in fine* (hereafter cited Naz); Brys, I, n. 376, 2°; Vromant, n. 30; Bouuaert-Simenon, I, n. 361.

[135] Crnica, I, p. 203; Ayrinhac, *General Legislation*, p. 366; Augustine, II, 188; Coronata, I, 290, 1°.

[136] Coronata, *loc. cit.;* Naz, I, n. 494, *in fine.*

[137] This canon does not refer to an extension of delegated power that is restricted to certain persons or to a definite place.—Cf. Coronata, I, n. 290, 1°, in nota 3, p. 343.

[138] Coronata, I, n. 290, 1°.

inadvertence (*actus per inadvertentiam positus*). Is one, therefore, to conclude that this exceptional provision can be used only once, and that subsequent inadvertent attempts would be rendered invalid? Such can hardly be the meaning of paragraph 2. In the first place, such a meaning is not expressly conveyed by the law, since it does not use a word that is exclusive. The law speaks of an act, but that is not the same as saying "only once" or "for one case." The word "*actus*" is used rather in the sense of "each act" without regard to the number of times or the period of time. Moreover, if it is restricted to but one case, this benign enactment would hardly avert the harm that is likely to result from the human defect of inadvertence.[139] Therefore, it may be held as certain that, as often as the inadvertence actually occurs when the one delegated for the internal forum is placing an act in the internal forum, that act will be valid in so far as the power of the delegate is concerned.

Article 3. *Cessante Causa Finali Delegationis*

Section I. Historical Note

A fourth way in which delegated power can cease is by the cessation of the final cause of the delegation.[140] Although the extinction of delegated power in this way is not anything new to the Code of Canon Law, it is of interest to note that this way is not listed among the causes effecting the cessation of delegation by even outstanding commentators of the earlier law. Of the authors consulted D'Annibale (1815-1892) was the first to separately list "*cessante causa finali*" among the phrases pointing to the causes extinguishing delegated power.[141] Other authors were found who, while not expressly employing any phrase like "*cessante causa finali,*" nevertheless under their treat-

[139] Toso, Lib. II, Tom. I, p. 177.

[140] Canon 207, § 1—"Potestas delegata extinguitur . . . cessante causa finali delegationis; . . . ."

[141] D'Annibale, I, n. 77.

ment of the subject, *completo mandato,* listed examples that are today commonly cited under the heading of cessation of the final cause.[142]

As the basis for this statement, D'Annibale cited a letter of Boniface VIII (1294-1303).[143] In this letter a bishop was ordered to provide a benefice for a poor cleric who, since he had none, was unable to maintain himself. But before the conferral could be made, the poor cleric obtained a benefice from some other source. Consequently the Pope ruled that, since the cause of the mandate had ceased, so had its effect.[144] The statement as made by D'Annibale, if one prescind from the word order, is verbatim reproduced in canon 207, § 1.

Section II. Canonical Commentary

In stating that delegated power is extinguished by the cessation of the final cause of the delegation, the legislator has in a terse manner enumerated a fourth way in which the extinguishing of delegated power can occur. And although the Code nowhere explains the meaning of *causa finalis,* the concept is beyond dispute. In this context of the Code, it is translated to mean the motive on account of which the power is transmitted to another.[145] Thus the use of the expression *causa finalis* harkens back to and

[142] Schmalzgrueber, lib. I, tit. XXIX, n. 41; Ojetti, *Synopsis Rerum Moralium et Iuris Pontificii* (3. ed., 4 vols., Romae, 1909-1914), s. v. *delegatio,* n. 1738 (hereafter cited Ojetti); Huth, lib. I, tit. XXIX, resp. 9, n. 4.

[143] C. 30, *de praebendis et dignitatibus,* III, 4, in VI°. Cf. D'Annibale, I, n. 77, in nota 57.

[144] *Glossa Ordinaria* ad c. 30, *eo. tit.,* III, 4, in VI°, s. v. *casus* and s. v. *cesset causa mandati.* In stating the *casus,* the glossator has also cited c. 60, X, *de appellationibus,* II, 28, to substantiate this jurisprudence.

[145] Ayrinhac, *General Legislation,* p. 367; Ramstein, *A Manual of Canon Law* (Hoboken, N. J.: Terminal Printing and Publishing Co., 1948), p. 167 (hereafter cited Ramstein); Augustine, II, 188; Eagleton, p. 45.

retains unchanged the traditional philosophical meaning of the word.

It is axiomatic to state that "every agent tends to some definite effect which is called to the end."[146] This end or final cause is that which is intended, or it may be called the reason prompting an agent to do something.[147] It is that which motivates or prompts an efficient cause to act.

Making application to the matter in hand, one must regard the grantor of the delegated power as the efficient cause, and the purpose on account of which he commissions another to act in his stead as the final cause. This purpose, moreover, is obviously an essential part of every act of delegation. The act of delegation, since it proceeds from a rational being, *ipso facto* presupposes a purpose. This purpose or end is, as Toso († 1946) designated it, the *anima mandati.*[148]

It is further to be observed that this final cause may be very general, as in the instance of the Quinquennial Faculties, or it may be particular, as in the delegation that enables someone to absolve from a censure. Further, the final cause may be singular, as in the example just cited, or there may be several purposes for the granting of the delegated power.

It should be clearly understood that the legislator is speaking of the final cause or the sufficient reason that prevails over anyone to delegate power to another. By exclusion, therefore, the cessation of a motive which is merely accidental or incidental, or, in other words, the subsiding of any and every impulsive cause (*causa impulsiva*) as such would not bring about the loss of delegated power.[149]

[146] St. Thomas Aquinas, *Summa contra Gentiles,* lib. III, c. 2 (Vivès ed., Vol. XII).

[147] St. Thomas Aquinas, *De Principiis Naturae* (Vivés ed., Vol. XXVII *Opuscula Varia,* pp. 480-486).

[148] Toso, Lib. II, Tom. I, p. 177.

[149] Cf. Prümmer, *Manuale Juris Canonici* (ed. 4. et 5., Friburgi Bris-

The reason assigned for the extinction of delegated power in consequence of the cessation of the final cause of the delegation varies. Lega-Bartoccetti reduce the cessation of the final cause to a tacit revocation of the delegation. Thus they reason that delegation directed to a certain end is understood as having been granted only within such limits. Accordingly when the end ceases, the will of the grantor tacitly revokes the power conferred.[150] On the other hand, Toso, whose view is more fundamental, preferred to assign as this reason the uselessness of delegated power which has lost its purpose. He designated the final cause as the *anima mandati.* When this *anima* ceases or dies, the power given by the said mandate, from the very nature of things, also ceases.[151]

The cessation of the final cause may occur because of several reasons. When the delegate has completed his commission, the final cause of his delegation automatically ceases by reason of the mandates fulfillment. Inasmuch as this instance is already provided for under the heading *"Expleto Mandato,"* it seems that the present enactment specifically refers to instances in which the final cause of the delegation itself is not actually fulfilled, but rather is broken off or made impossible of fulfillment. For example, delegation is given to Father James in order to absolve John from a censure. In the meantime suppose that the censure has been removed by someone else, or suppose that John has died. The purpose of Father James' delegated power, therefore, is made impossible of fulfillment. The final cause of the delegation having ceased, the delegated power suffers the same effect. Or again, delegation

goviae, 1927), p. 123 (hereafter cited Prümmer). By analogy to the cause prompting the concession of a dispensation, cf. Van Hove, *Commentarium Lovaniense in Codicem Iuris Canonici,* Vol. I, Tomus V, *De Privilegiis, De Dispensationibus* (Mechliniae-Romae: H. Dessain, 1939), n. 492 (hereafter cited *De Priv.-De Disp.*).

150 Lega-Bartoccetti, I, p. 203.

151 Toso, Lib. II, Tom. I, p. 177; Kinane, "Jurisdiction in the New Code," *The Irish Ecclesiastical Record,* 5. series, XIII (1919), 216.

is given to Father Albert to hear a case and render a judicial sentence. Suppose that before he has begun hearing the case, or even during the hearing of it, the parties have settled the controversy by way of compromise. This compromise removes the purpose of the delegation and brings about its cessation.

One may raise the question whether the cessation of the final cause must be total before it can serve to extinguish the power delegated, or whether for the same effect it need be only a partial cessation. This question seems to suppose either a general final cause, aspects of which could cease, or an instance in which there are two or more final causes, of which one at least ceases. That these suppositions cover the case may be argued from the observation that the word *cessare* does not seem to admit the alternate state of half-existing and half-ceasing. The final cause, when it is singular, either exists or does not exist. But, moreover, this same reasoning seems applicable even when the final cause is general or when it is multiple. So long as a general final cause or a multiple final cause has not totally ceased, the utility of the delegation or the *anima mandati* is present, and therefore the delegated power continues (from the viewpoint of an attendant final cause) to exist. That the cessation of the final cause must be total is the unanimous teaching of the commentators.[152]

While an abundance of extrinsic proof is at hand to establish the necessity of the *total* cessation of the final cause, the other extreme obtains relative to the *certain* or *doubtful* cessation of the final cause. Toso, for one,

[152] Toso, Lib. II, Tom. I, p. 177; Wernz-Vidal, II, n. 377, 3°; Brys, I, n. 376, 3°; Romani, I, n. 324; Maroto, I, n. 715, II; Jone, *Commentarium in Codicem Iuris Canonici,* Vol. I (Paderborn: Officina Libraria F. Schöningh, 1950), p. 207 (hereafter cited Jone); Coronata, I, n. 290, 3°; Regatillo, I, n. 367; Cappello, *Tractatus Canonico-Moralis de Sacramentis* (5 vols., Augustae Taurinorum Romae: Domus Editorialis Marietti. Vol. II, *De Poenitentia,* 4. ed., 1944; Vol. V, *De Matrimonio,* 5. ed., 1947), V, n. 255 (hereafter cited *De Sacramentis*).

was found to maintain explicitly that the delegated power ceases when it is certain that the final cause is lacking.[153] This is tantamount to holding that in case of doubt the delegation remains. This view is tenable, for just as the concession of delegated power is a fact that is not presumed, but rather must be proved, so also the extinction of that power is not to be presumed.

If the *total* cessation of the final cause is emphasized, a question arises when one adverts to the possibility of a reviving of the final cause. Does the word *"cessante,"* which is interpreted as connoting a total cessation, mean that the final cause must have ceased in such a way as to exclude the possibility of its recurrence or revival in the same case? Or does it mean simply that, according to a prudent judgment and the sense of the rescript of delegation, the purpose of the delegation has indeed ceased, though because of supervening circumstances there may reoccur a similar final cause? In other words, what effect does the revival of the final cause have upon delegated power? As an instance, consider the example given above. Suppose that delegation is given for the hearing of a case and the passing of a judicial sentence, and in the meantime an amicable agreement is reached. This amicable agreement (in the canonical sense of canons 1925-1932) extinguishes the delegated power.[154] If subsequently the matter is brought back into court, would a new grant of delegated power be necessary, or would the former delegated power revive?

The revival of delegated power by reason of the revival of the final cause of the delegation does not seem to have any legal basis. Canon 207, § 1 enacts the extinction of the delegated power through the very cessation of the final cause, which cause alone sustains the continued existence of that power. No provision is made in the Code for such an automatic re-conferral of the dele-

153 Toso, Lib. II, Tom. I, p. 177.

154 Crnica, I, p. 203; Ramstein, p. 167; Blat, I, n. 156.

gated power. Consequently, even though the final cause should by reason of supervening circumstances have become re-existent, a new grant of delegation would be necessitated.

Using the example just given, one may ask what effect would be had if at the time of the compromise the case were no longer integral in respect to the exercise of delegated authority? Would the delegated power be extended to the case if it were re-introduced into court? Chelodi and Romani seem to maintain, not precisely that the delegated power would be extended or that it would revive, but that it had never ceased. They qualify the required cessation of the final cause with the notion of integral or untouched matter.[155] No explanation or examples are given by them. Surely they do not mean to limit the application of the clause *cessante causa finali* simply to matters that are integral, so that once the delegate has begun to use the delegated power, it could not cease by the cessation of the final cause. This meaning would put an unreasonable and unnecessary restriction on the words of the canon.

Besides, in some cases this interpretation would leave the cessation of delegated power unexplained, and allow the delegated power to continue, evidently without sufficient reason or purpose. For example, delegated power is given for the dispensing of Titus from a matrimonial impediment to enable him to marry Caia. If Titus should die after the delegate had begun the jurisdictional exercise of his power, but before the dispensation was granted, then the continuance of the delegate's authority would manifestly be purposeless, and yet the cessation of his power would not be explained.[156] If the qualification by Chelodi and

[155] Chelodi, n. 129—"Delegati iurisdictio expirat . . . cessante causa finali delegationis, scilicet antequam ea delegatus usus sit; . . . ."

Romani, I, n. 324—"Delegata potestas extinguitur . . . cessante causa finali delegationis, equidem totaliter, adaequate, re integra; . . . ."

[156] D'Annibale (I, n. 77, in nota 76), Crnica (I, p. 203) and Wernz-Vidal (II, n. 377, 3°) cite this example without distinguishing whether or not the matter is integral.

Romani means that the delegated power revives if perchance the final cause becomes re-existent, then the application of the clause *cessante causa finali* would look solely to those cases in which the final cause has irrevocably ceased beyond all possibility of a revival. The example just cited would be an instance. The physical death of Titus would irrevocably extinguish the final cause of the delegated power. But this meaning seems unwarranted, if not unreasonable, and appears to exceed the limits of the obvious sense of the words of the Code.

In the article "*Elapso Tempore*" it was held that, once the delegate had put his hand to the matter assigned, generally he could by reason of that fact bring the matter to a valid conclusion, even though he acted beyond the designated time. In the present consideration, the question of *res integra* does not seem applicable. It is the cessation of the final cause that reduces delegated power to extinction. That is accomplished regardless of whether or not the matter had been given a legal turn (*re non amplius integra*).

CHAPTER IV

CESSATION BY REASON OF THE PERSON DELEGATING

Within the purview of the present chapter is to be considered any cessation of delegated power which is effected by reason of an act or condition of the delegator. This active subject of delegated power is, of course, either one with ordinary power, which power is not inhibited with reference to delegation, or one with delegated power who is authorized by law or by special grant to further delegate (subdelegate) the power conferred.

He who has ordinary power is capable of delegating his power totally or partially, unless there is an express provision to the contrary.[1] Moreover, a person who fills the office of delegate of the Holy See is empowered to further delegate such delegated power either habitually or for a particular case unless that person is commissioned because of personal qualities or unless subdelegation is prohibited.[2] Power delegated *ad uni-*

[1] Canon 199, § 1—"Qui iurisdictionis potestatem habet ordinariam, potest eam alteri ex toto vel ex parte delegare, nisi aliud expresse iure caveatur." For examples of exceptions cf. canons 239, § 1, 1°; 401, § 1; 874, § 1; 1096, § 1; and a response *Comm. Intr. Cod.*, 16 oct. 1919, ad 3—*AAS*, XI (1919), 496. Noone indicates some persons who are unable to delegate jurisdiction. He says that the vicar-general cannot delegate judicial jurisdiction, since ordinarily he himself does not possess it (canon 1573, § 1). It is seriously doubted whether the *officialis* can delegate his power either entirely or partially, i.e., in the sense that the delegated judge would decide the case and pronounce the sentence. Arguing from canon 1607 and from extrinsic authority, he maintains that the safer opinion is the negative one. Cf. *Nullity in Judicial Acts*, The Catholic University of America Canon Law Studies, n. 297 (Washington, D. C.: The Catholic University of America Press, 1950), pp. 21-22 (hereafter cited Noone).

[2] Canon 199, § 2—"Etiam potestas iurisdictionis ab Apostolica Sede delegata subdelegari potest sive ad actum, sive etiam habitualiter, nisi electa fuerit industria personae aut subdelegatio prohibita."

versitatem causarum by one who intermediately to the Roman Pontiff holds ordinary power, can indeed be subdelegated, but only for individual cases.[3] When delegation is given only for individual cases, then jurisdictional acts can be further delegated only if an express provision to that effect is made.[4] Subdelegated power cannot be further transferred to another unless an express provision has been made to that effect.[5]

With this legislation in mind, the present chapter considers the extinction of delegated or subdelegated power by reason of the one delegating. The Code supplies the basis for a dividing of this chapter into two articles.

ARTICLE 1. *Revocatione Delegantis*

The Code provides for the cessation of delegated power because of its revocation by the one delegating, which act of revocation, to be effective, must be directly intimated to the delegate.[6]

Section I. Historical Note

The text most frequently cited for the revocation of delegated power is found in the Rules of Law of Gregory IX (1227-1241), wherein it is stated that things are dissolved by the same causes that brought them about.[7] Other texts of the Decretal Law clearly establish that the cessation

[3] Canon 199, § 3—"Potestas delegata ad universitatem negotiorum ab eo qui infra Romanum Pontificem habet ordinariam potestatem, potest in singulis casibus subdelegari."

[4] Canon 199, § 4—"In aliis casibus potestas iurisdictionis delegata subdelegari potest tantummodo ex concessione expresse facta, sed articulum aliquem non iurisdictionalem etiam sine expressa commissione iudices delegati possunt subdelegare."

[5] Canon 199, § 5—"Nulla subdelegata potestas potest iterum subdelegari, nisi id expresse concessum fuerit." Cf. Bastnagel, "Authorization of the Further Committing of Subdelegated Power," *The Jurist*, IX (1949), 412-414.

[6] Canon 207, § 1—"Potestas delegata extinguitur ... revocatione delegantis delegato directe intimata. ..."

[7] C. 1, X, *de regulis iuris*, V, 41: "Omnis res, per quascunque causas nascitur, per easdem dissolvitur." Cf. Sanchez, lib. III, disp. XXXVI, n. 13; D'Annibale, I, n. 77, in nota 59; Cocchi, Lib. II, Pars I, p. 246.

of delegated power because of revocation was in institute of pre-Code legislation. For example, Innocent III (1198-1216) delineated the procedure to be followed when delegation was granted successively to two persons.[8] A letter of delegation was given to a priest, who held the rank of *primicerius* and *plebanus,* to settle a controversy. Subsequently a second letter of delegation was given to an archpriest in the diocese of Padua. The Pope was asked to determine which one possessed the delegated power. It was decided that if the second letter expressly made mention of the first, the delegated power of the second would stand, since the power of the first had thus been revoked.[9]

This response of Innocent III and the other citations in the footnotes seem to refer only to express revocation. Whether or not the revocation had to be made expressly (in the sense of direct intimation) to the delegate does not seem to be enunciated. Nor is the fact of, or the necessity of, intimation brought out in the Constitutions of Innocent XIII (1721-1724)[10] or Benedict XIV (1740-1758),[11] which speak of the revocation of confessional jurisdiction. Nevertheless Van Hove (1872-1947) stated that the necessity of direct intimation was the *"communior doctrina"* even before the Code.[12]

[8] C. 29, X, *de officio et potestate iudicis delegati,* I, 29; Potthast, n. 325. Cf. also c. 24, X, *de rescriptis,* I, 3; Potthast, n. 4072; c. 28, § 2, X, *de officio et potestate iudicis delegati,* I, 29; Potthast, n. 2350; cc. 6, 7, *eo. tit.,* I, 14, in VI°.

[9] *Glossa Ordinaria* ad c. 29, X, *eo. tit.,* I, 29, s. *Casus.* Cf. also c. 3, X, *de rescriptis,* I, 3; Jaffé, n. 9226; c. 14, *eo. tit.,* I, 3; Potthast, n. 2350; *Glossa Ordinaria* ad c. 30, X, *de officio et potestate iudicis delegati,* I, 29, s. v. *Re integra.*

[10] Cf. Innocent XIII, const. *Apostolici ministerii,* 23 maii 1723, § 19—*Fontes,* n. 280.

[11] Cf. Benedict XIV, const. *In supremo,* 23 sept. 1724, § 16—*Fontes,* n. 283; const. *Apostolica indulta,* 5 aug. 1744, § 3—*Fontes,* n. 344.

[12] Van Hove, *De Rescr.,* n. 288. In the same place he cited Suarez (Vol. 5, lib. III, c. 40, nn. 6-7) for one, as holding that direct intimation was not necessary. Suarez held that the extinction of delegated power

Section II. Canonical Commentary

The terminology of the Code has concisely restated the pre-Code jurisprudence relative to the revocation of delegated power. Canon 207, § 1 legislates that delegated power is extinguished by revocation made by the delegator and directly intimated to the delegate.

The term *revocation* comes from the Latin *revocare* and means an act of recalling or taking back. However, as a canonical institute, revocation may be considered from the viewpoint of the revocatory act itself and from the viewpoint of the legal effectiveness of this act. The first may be called revocation *in actu primo*; the latter, which stresses the notion of intimation, may be designated as revocation *in actu secundo. In actu primo,* therefore, revocation is an act of the will on the part of the grantor that countermands what he earlier handed over to another. Just as the concession required an act on the part of the grantor, so also does the revocation require a new act on the part of the grantor. However, the merely extant revocatory will of the grantor is legally insufficient; its efficacy *in actu secundo* depends on a direct intimation to the grantee.

The act of revocation can be either express or tacit, as is indicated by the unmodified terminology of canon 207, § 1, namely, *revocatione delegantis,*[13] and by an analogous

occurred so long as some knowledge of the revocation was had by the delegate. Pichler (lib. I, tit. XXIX, n. 19) held that intimation must be made in some manner. Gonzalez-Tellez (lib. I, tit. XXIX, c. XX, n. 9) merely said that the delegate needed knowledge of the revocation in order that it be effective.

[13] Lega-Bartoccetti, I, p. 203. See also Schmalzgrueber, lib. I, tit. XXIX, n. 45; Huth, lib. I, tit. XXIX, resp. 9, n. 2; Sebastianelli, *De Personis,* pars 1, n. 126, c. Two authors were found to hold the contrary. Cf. Coronata, I, n. 290, 4°, who follows Augustine, II, 189. Their interpretation arises from a failure to distinguish the act of revocation from the intimation of it. The law does not say that the revocation must be express, but only that the intimation must be direct. Tacit revocation does not exclude the possibility of direct intimation.

consideration of the revocation of rescripts.[14] Express revocation is that which by words or writing clearly and formally manifests the revocatory will of the delegator; tacit is that which by some fact implies that the grantor's will is recalled.[15] Moreover, just as power can be totally or partially delegated, so also can the act of revocation be directed toward the entire delegation or only a part of it. It should also be remembered that the revocation of delegated power is a juridic fact which is not to be presumed. Once delegated power is transferred to the delegate, it is not presumed to be extinguished.

Potestas delegata extinguitur . . . revocatione. . . . From these unrestricted words it is indisputable that every delegated power, whether it derives *a lege* or *ab homine,* or whether it has been granted *ad universitatem causarum* or *in singulis casibus,* is subject to the law of revocation. Indeed, juridically this derives from the law itself. The legislator, however, has simply stated what follows *ex natura* from a concession of delegated power.[16] Such a concession is certainly a participation in the power of another. As a power it has not been transferred in the sense that the delegator has lost or relinquished his own right.[17]

The right to recall the granted power is presupposed in every concession emanating from ordinary power, since such a delegator possesses power *suo iure* and *re propria.*[18] Thus

[14] Canon 60. Cf. Van Hove, *De Rescr.*, n. 286; Michiels, II, 470-471. The contrary is held by Cicognani, p. 770.

[15] Van Hove, *De Rescr.*, n. 286; Brys, I, n. 258.

[16] Icard, *Praelectiones Juris Canonici* (3 vols., Lutetiae Parisiorum, 1859), I, n. 274, I (hereafter cited Icard).

[17] Suarez, Vol. 22, disp. XXVI, sect. III, n. 1. Note that this statement does not say that a delegated power cannot be relinquished, as shall be seen when consideration is given to a delegate who has totally subdelegated his power to another and the matter has been undertaken by the subdelegate.

[18] Schmalzgrueber, lib. I, tit. XXIX, n. 45; Ferraris, *Prompta Bibliotheca Canonica, Juridica, Moralis, Theologica, necnon Ascetica, Polemica, Rubricistica, Historica* (ed. novissima, 9 vols., Romae, 1885-1899), s. v. *delegare*, n. 56 (hereafter cited Ferraris); Bargilliat, *Prae-*

the statement that a delegated power is a gratuitous power and as such depends entirely on the will of the grantor[19] is applicable to all delegated power from the point of view of its concession. The statement is also applicable, from the point of view of revocation, to a grantor acting in virtue of ordinary power, and also to a grantor acting in virtue of delegated power, provided the delegate retains some right over the power he has subdelegated.[20] It seems that the preservation of the right of the delegator is the basis or the principle in virtue of which revocation may be accomplished.

The Code uses the phrase *revocatione* DELEGANTIS. Who may place the acts that are required if there is to be effected the revocation of a delegated power? At first sight, it may obviously be stated that he who has granted the power has the right to recall it. This general statement is unconditionally applicable to a grantor endowed with ordinary power. He may revoke, as he sees proper, the delegated power which he has given. Moreover, in the instance of a concession made in virtue of ordinary power, whoever succeeds to that ordinary power may likewise revoke the power that had been granted to another by the predecessor.[21] It appears that the Rule of Law, "*Is, qui in ius succedit alterius, eo iure, quo ille, uti debebit,*" is fully applicable here.[22] Besides the delegator and his successor, it is reasonable that their superior relative to the matter delegated likewise possesses the right to revoke the power granted by the inferior.[23] Moreover, according to

lectiones Juris Canonici (37. ed., ad canones novi Codicis redacta, 2 vols., Parisiis, 1923-1924), I, 248 (hereafter cited Bargilliat).

19 Suarez, Vol. 22, disp. XXVI, sect. III, n. 1; Sanchez, lib. III, disp. XXVI, n. 8; Pichler, lib. I, tit. XXIX, n. 19; Brys, I, n. 376, 4°.

20 Cf. *infra*, pp. 72-74.

21 Gasparri, *Tractatus Canonicus de Matrimonio* (2 vols., ed. nova ad mentem Codicis I. C., Romae: Typis Polyglottis Vaticanis, 1932), II, n. 958 (hereafter cited Gasparri); De Meester, I, n. 475; Brys, I, n. 376, 4°.

22 Reg. 46, R. J., in VI°.

23 Brys, *loc. cit.*

the principles of delegation, it is possible for any of these to delegate someone to undertake the revocation of the delegated power.[24] The authority of the one delegated for the revoking of a delegated power could, of course, be circumscribed with various limitations.[25]

The right of revoking a power that has been granted to another is likewise enjoyed by a delegate who has subdelegated his commission. The right of this delegate, however, is not absolute; for its closer specification it depends on whether or not the delegate has kept at least a partial control over the power that he has subdelegated to another.[26]

From the statement of canon 207, § 1, it is evident that revocation *in actu primo* is legally insufficient to effect the cessation of delegated power. The revocatory will of the delegator must be directly intimated to the delegate. Van Hove rightly observed that this legislation of the Code is in agreement with the pre-Code jurisprudence.[27] It was held expressly by such outstanding canonists as Reiffenstuel (1642-1703)[28] and Wernz (1842-1914),[29] and also Giraldus (1692-1775)[30] and D'Annibale (1815-1892).[31] This intimation or apprisal of the situation to the delegate or the subdelegate, as the case may be, is necessary in order that the act of revocation have effect.[32] Hence acts placed by the delegate after the act of revocation but be-

[24] Canon 199, § 1. Cf. Blat, II, n. 156, 4°, though his statement here seems somewhat ambiguous.

[25] Canon 203.

[26] This teaching is founded upon the pre-Code law.—Cf. c. 6, *de officio et potestate iudicis delegati*, I, 14, in VI°; c. 37, X, *eo. tit.*, I, 29; Potthast, n. 7762.

[27] Van Hove, *De Rescr.*, n. 288, in nota 1, p. 266.

[28] Reiffenstuel, lib. I, tit. XXIX, n. 141.

[29] Wernz, II, n. 561, VII.

[30] Giraldus, *Animadversiones et Additamenta ad A. Barbosa de Officio et Potestate Parochi* (Romae, 1831), pars II, cap. XXI, n. 67.

[31] D'Annibale, I, n. 77, 3°.

[32] Reiffenstuel, lib. I, tit. XXIX, n. 141; Icard, I, n. 274, I; Kearney, p. 115.

fore the intimation of that act of revocation are valid.[33] The revocatory will of the grantor must be externalized and brought to the attention of the delegate.

Any pre-Code dispute relative to the intimation is now academic. The law is explicit in requiring a direct intimation (*directe intimata*). The meaning of the word *directe* seems to be beyond dispute. It should be noted that in the statement of canon 207, § 1 on revocation, the word *directe* is used not in conjunction with the act of revocation by the delegator, but rather in description of how the intimation is to be made to the delegate. Hence the delegate's knowledge of the fact that the act of revocation has occurred must be direct.

The term *directe* does not mean to imply that the delegator must personally convey to the delegate the fact of revocation. This apprisal can be expedited through a messenger or a procurator or, if the delegator prefers, *viva voce* or by a letter narrating the fact.[34] Toso († 1946) interpreted *directe* to mean that the intimation needed to be made to the person of the delegate.[35] While it is conceded that knowledge of the act of revocation must be transmitted to the person of the delegate, it seems that the first and obvious meaning of the word *directe* calls for it as being synonymous with the word "officially."[36] Thus the intimation of the act of revocation is sufficiently transmitted whenever official information is obtained by the delegate. Until such official information is obtained, the acts performed in virtue of delegated power are vested with

[33] D'Annibale, I, n. 77, in nota 60; Cappello, *Summa*, I, n. 258, 4°.

[34] Beste, p. 221; Coronata, I, n. 290, 4°; Vermeersch-Creusen, I, n. 322, 4°; Brys, I, n. 376, 4°, in nota 1. Whether official notice in the diocesan newspaper could be used is not considered by authors. It seems probable that this means could be used for an intimating of the revocatory will of the delegator, especially if revocation is made by way of the promulgation of a contrary law (cf. canon 60, § 2).

[35] Toso, Lib. II, Tom. I, p. 176.

[36] Regatillo, I, n. 367, d; Prümmer, p. 123; Wernz, II, n. 561, VII; Lega-Bartoccetti, I, p. 203; Kinane, "Jurisdiction in the New Code," *The Irish Ecclesiastical Record*, 5. series, XIII (1919), 216.

validity. The necessity of the conveying of official information to the delegate is based by analogy on the necessity of official notification regarding the grant of the delegated power.[37] Negatively, therefore, direct intimation implies that the delegate's knowledge must not be obtained in some casual manner or by way of rumor.[38] This source of knowledge would be legally ineffective.

The canonical reason for requiring direct intimation seems to be the prevention of detriment to the community.[39] If the act of revocation alone sufficed, there could always arise the uncertainty about the existence of the delegate's power, and hence the uncertainty concerning the acts placed by him. One would not know whether perchance the delegate's power had been recalled.

Canon 207, § 1 does not state that a revocation can be made by the delegator only before the delegate has begun to use the power conferred.[40] The requisite, as stated, is a revocation which must be directly intimated. *Ubi lex non distinguit, nec nos distinguere debemus.* Therefore, relative to the question of the *res integra,* the general principle based on the fundamental right of the delegator may be formulated as follows. In every instance in which power remains radically founded in the delegator, that power as shared with another can be recalled. This statement seems to provide for every contingency.

One with ordinary power radically retains power even though it is delegated *ad universitatem causarum* to another. Therefore it always remains within the competence of one with ordinary power to recall whatever power he has transferred to another.[41]

[37] Canon 53. Cf. Reiffenstuel, lib. I, tit. XXIX, n. 141; Maroto, I, n. 713, II; Bargilliat, I, 248.

[38] Gasparri, II, n. 985; Chelodi, n. 129.

[39] Icard, n. 274, I; Reiffenstuel, lib. I, tit. XXIX, n. 141.

[40] O'Neill incorrectly injects the clause "before the execution had been started." Cf. p. 195.

[41] Reiffenstuel, lib. I, tit. XXIX, n. 136; Maroto, I, n. 713, II, 1°; Wernz-Vidal, II, n. 377, 4°.

One who enjoys delegated power *ad universitatem causarum,* whether the source of that power be the Holy See or one inferior to the Holy See, is considered in many respects as one with ordinary power.[42] The Code of Canon Law indicates this by conferring upon such a delegate the power of subdelegating,[43] which in all other delegations is ordinarily precluded.[44] Moreover, the Code has established the same principle of interpretation for both ordinary power and power delegated universally.[45] Hence, although the Code has no express statement as to the inherent firmness of power delegated *ad universitatem causarum vel negotiorum,* nevertheless it seems fully acceptable to maintain that such power enjoys greater stability than power delegated for a particular case. Accordingly it further seems soundly legal that one with power delegated *ad universitatem causarum,* in the event of a legitimate subdelegation, is able at any time to recall that subdelegation.[46] In other words, unlike particular delegation, as will be seen, universal delegation is not abdicated by its subdelegation.[47]

A universal delegate of one subordinate to the Roman Pontiff is incapable of abdicating, since he is legally disqualified from subdelegating except in single cases.[48] From this point of view, therefore, he always retains part of his jurisdiction and consequently is competent to revoke

[42] Maroto, I, n. 705, D, p. 844; Brys, I, n. 371; Coronata, I, n. 288, 1°, b.

[43] Canon 199, §§ 2, 3. Exception, of course, is made for one selected in view of the *industria personae* and for delegation given with a clause prohibiting subdelegation.

[44] Canan 199, §§ 4, 5.

[45] Canon 200, § 1—"Potestas iurisdictionis ordinaria et ad universitatem negotiorum delegata, late interpretanda est; alia quaelibet stricte; . . . ."

[46] Kearney, p. 115.

[47] The term *abdication* is used with reference to a particular delegate who has totally subdelegated the power conferred to himself and the matter has been undertaken at the hand of the subdelegate.

[48] Canon 199, § 3.

the subdelegated power despite the fact that the matter has been given a legal turn (*res non amplius integra*) by his subdelegate.

A universal delegate of the Holy See is likewise unable to abdicate. Although empowered to subdelegate even habitually such a delegate does not abdicate by totally subdelegating his power when that is possible. The clearest confirmation of this is found in fact. The local ordinary of a diocese is granted universal (in a relative sense) delegation in the form of Quinquennial Faculties. He may subdelegate his chancellor to expedite all matrimonial dispensations for mixed religion or disparity of cult.[49] No one will maintain that the local ordinary is unable to recall this faculty, any more than that the Holy See is unable to revoke the delegation given to the local ordinary.[50]

The competence of the universal delegate to recall his subdelegation in every case is not enjoyed by a particular delegate, whether of the Holy See or of one subordinate to the Holy See.[51] Although the present legislation is silent on this point, the constant teaching of the canonists since the time of the Decretal Law seems to obtain today.[52]

[49] Prince, *The Diocesan Chancellor*, The Catholic University of America Canon Law Studies, n. 167 (Washington, D. C.: The Catholic University of America Press, 1942), pp. 107-108.

[50] The pre-Code extraordinary faculties enjoyed by the bishops of the United States ceased in this manner. Cf. S. C. Consist., decr. *Proxima sacra*, 25 apr. 1918—*AAS*, X (1918), 190. See Motry, *Diocesan Faculties according to the Code of Canon Law*, The Catholic University of America Canon Law Studies, n. 16 (Washington, D. C.: The Catholic University of America, 1922), p. 39 (hereafter cited Motry).

[51] Kearney (p. 115) was the only author found to make expressly this distinction between universal and particular delegates. The others merely state that when a delegate totally hands over his power, and it is given a legal turn by the subdelegate, the power is no longer revocable by the hand of the delegate.

[52] Wernz-Vidal, II, n. 377, 4°; Coronata, I, n. 290, 4°, in nota 10, p. 343.

Decretal Law clearly taught that the subdelegation of delegated power became efficaciously transferred to the subdelegate as soon as the subdelegate undertook the (sub-) commission.[53] It further taught that the delegate on his part irrevocably handed over his power when he totally (*simpliciter*) subdelegated the case committed to him and the case was given a legal turn by the subdelegate.[54] Ferraris († c. 1763) indicated the reason why this result obtains. The delegate who entirely hands over to another the case committed to himself, by not reserving any power to himself, loses control over it when the power becomes efficaciously transferred to the subdelegate by use at the hand of the subdelegate.[55] When the delegate so acts, he is said to have abdicated his position as a delegate, and therefore loses his power.[56] Coronata reasons that the delegate has fulfilled his office by totally commissioning another to undertake the matter delegated to himself.[57]

Though it might seem that the power of the delegate should be perpetuated in the delegate through the act of subdelegation, Passerinus (1594-1677) pointed out that the act of subdelegating does not connote a use of the delegated power as such. Even if the act of subdelegating were a use of delegated power, it would not perpetuate delegated jurisdiction in the one delegating or give the delegated matter a legal turn, thus sealing the delegate's possession and control in the matter, because the act of

[53] C. 6, *de officio et potestate iudicis delegati,* I, 14, in VI°; c. 37, X, *eo. tit.*, I, 29; Potthast, n. 7762.

[54] *Glossa Ordinaria* ad c. 27, § 3, X, *eo. tit.*, I, 29, s. v. Vices suas; ad c. 37, X, *eo. tit.*, I, 29, s. vv. *Vices suas* and *Non potuit demandare;* ad c. 6, *eo. tit.*, I, 14, in VI°, s. v. *In totum.*

[55] Ferraris, s. v. *delegare*, n. 56, 5°. Cf. also *Glossa Ordinaria* ad c. 27, § 2, X, *eo. tit.*, I, 29, s. v. *Transfert.* For post-Code authors cf. Brys, I, n. 376, 4°; Cocchi, Lib. II, Pars I, p. 246; Toso, Lib. II, Tom. I, p. 177; Wernz-Vidal, II, p. 377, 4°.

[56] Pirhing, lib. I, tit. XXIX, n. 155; Wernz-Vidal, II, n. 377, 4°; Kearney, p. 115.

[57] Coronata, I, n. 290, 4°.

subdelegating does not directly touch the case or matter delegated to himself.[58]

Relative to the question concerning the *res integra,* Kearney ably summarizes the present legislation when he states the following:

> "It is to be noted that the ordinary Superior, as well as the universal delegate, may recall his mandate at any time. On the other hand, the particular delegate who has legitimately subdelegated the power given to him for a particular case, cannot recall his power, once the subdelegate has begun to act. He may, however, recall his mandate, if he has retained to himself some portion of the power originally committed to him, since in this case he has not abdicated."[59]

The question may be raised whether a cause is necessary either for the validity of the revocation or for its lawfulness. From what has been said about the right of the active subject of delegation, it is immediately obvious that in no case in which a revocation is possible is a cause necessary for the validity of the revocation.[60] The necessity of a cause for the validity of the revocation seems to be nowhere demanded by law, neither in canon 207, § 1, nor in the analogous canon 60 concerning the revocation of rescripts,[61] nor in canon 880, §§ 1, 3 relative to the revocation of jurisdiction for the hearing of confessions.[62]

[58] Passerinus, lib. I, *de officio et potestate iudicis delegati,* c. VI, n. 22. He states the alternative reason here because his opinion on the first point is not unanimously held. He cited Hostiensis and Ioannes Andreae as opposed.

[59] Kearney, p. 115.

[60] Maroto, I, n. 713, II, 2°; Coronata, I, n. 290, 4°; Wernz-Vidal, II, n. 377, 4°.

[61] Roelker, *Principles of Privileges according to the Code of Canon Law,* The Catholic University of America Canon Law Studies, n. 35 (Washington, D. C.: The Catholic University of America, 1926), pp. 104-105 (hereafter cited Roelker).

[62] It is disputed whether in canon 880, §§ 1, 3, a just cause is required for validity. The negative opinion seems to have the greater probability. Cf. Vermeersch-Creusen, II, n. 150; Cappello, *De Sacramentis,* II, n. 293; Coronata, *Institutiones Iuris Canonici de Sacra-*

However, it is unanimously taught that a just cause is needed in order that the act of revocation be rendered licit.[63] This conclusion seems to be particularly applicable in an instance of revocation made by the superior of the delegator, since then the power of the delegator to commission another would be all but nullified.[64] The just cause that exists for the revoking of the delegated power need not, of course, be indicated to the delegate.[65]

It can be observed also that since the delegation depends entirely upon the will of the grantor, his revocation of the delegated power does not violate any right of the delegate. Hence there is not established any basis for an appeal.[66] Whatever recourse remains open, it is such that, if invoked, it is not attended with any suspensive effect.

ARTICLE 2. *Resoluto Iure Delegantis*

By reason of the active subject or the delegator, the legislator has formulated in a negative way the general principle that delegated power does not cease by the dissolution of the right of the delegator.[67] It is by way of exception that the cessation of delegated power is accomplished when a clause to that effect appears in the delegation, or when the rescript confers to some individual the power to grant a favor to particular persons mentioned

mentis, (3 vols., Vol. I, Taurini-Romae: Domus Editorialis Marietti, 1943), n. 357; Cocchi, Lib. II, Pars I, p. 246.

[63] Coronata, I, n. 290, 4°; Brys, I, n. 376, 4°; *et alii.* Pre-Code authors disputed this. Sanchez (lib. III, disp. XXXIII, nn. 6-7) and Suarez (Vol. 22, disp. XXVI, sect. III, n. 3) held that basically no cause was needed even with a view to lawfulness. The better opinion held that a just cause was necessary for the lawfulness, not however for the validity. Cf. Wernz, II, n. 561, VII; Aertnys, *Theologia Moralis* (7. ed., 2 vols., Paderbornae, 1906), II, n. 231.

[64] Suarez (Vol. 22, disp. XXVI, sect. III, n. 3; Vol. 6, lib. VIII, c. XXXVII, n. 17) held that such a revocation would be invalid if made by anyone subordinate to the Holy See.

[65] Brys, I, n. 376, 4°.

[66] Brys, *loc. cit.*

[67] Canon 207, § 1—"Potestas delegata extinguitur . . . non autem resoluto iure delegantis, nisi in duobus casibus de quibus in can. 61."

in the rescript and the one who has such power under the rescript has not yet begun to use it when the delegator lost his right.[68]

Section I. Historical Note

In Decretal Law one is able to find the historical basis for all the present legislation. Boniface VIII (1294-1303) ordained that, if the Roman Pontiff granted a favor with the proviso *ad suae voluntatis beneplacitum,* such a favor ceased by his death, since death entirely extinguished his *beneplacitum;* whereas, if the grant was made *ad Apostolicae Sedis beneplacitum,* the favor endured even after the death of the Pope.[69]

In another place the same Pope wrote that when power, e.g. to confer benefices, was granted as a favor to some individual without any designation of the persons to be assigned, it remained permanent even when the matter was integral, despite the death of its grantor; however, if power was given with the proviso that a specified person be appointed, that power ceased entirely with the demise of the grantor of the power when the matter envisioned in the use of the power was still intact.[70] Pope Boniface further stated that even if the matter was wholly intact, the executor of a rescript containing a favor that had already been granted (*gratia facta*) could execute it even after the death of the Pope.[71]

Another general principle enunciated by Lucius III (1181-1185) as well as by Urban III (1185-1187) and Innocent III (1198-1216) maintained that a delegated judge lost his power if he had not begun to act before the death of

[68] Canon 61—"Per Apostolicae Sedis aut dioecesis vacationem nullum eiusdem Sedis Apostolicae aut Ordinarii rescriptum perimitur, nisi aliud ex additis clausulis appareat, aut rescriptum contineat potestatem alicui factam concedendi gratiam peculiaribus personis in eodem expressis, et res adhuc integra sit."

[69] C. 5, *de rescriptis,* I, 3, in VI°.

[70] C. 36, *de praebendis et dignitatibus,* III, 4, in VI°.

[71] C. 9, *de officio et potestate iudicis delegati,* I, 14, in VI°.

the grantor.[72] As the canonical commentary unfolds, the application of these provisions will become evident.

Section II. Canonical Commentary

Through canon 61, canon 207, § 1 treats of the cessation of delegated jurisdiction as consequent upon the physical or juridical death of the delegator. In the two exceptions advanced through canon 61 when treating of the cessation of rescripts, the extinction of delegated power is effected automatically, so that when an exceptive clause appears in the letter of delegation, or when the delegated power is given for the purpose that a favor may be granted to determined persons and the commission has not been undertaken by the delegate, the death of the delegator *ipso facto* extinguishes the power of the delegate.[73] From this it should be emphasized again and again that the general rule substantiates the preservation of the delegated power despite the physical or legal demise of the grantor.[74]

In relation to the two exceptions, canon 207, § 1 states without any modifying clauses that delegated power ceases when the delegator loses his right (*resoluto iure delegantis*). This right or power of the delegator can be lost in various ways, e.g. by physical death, by renunciation, by removal from office, by transfer to another office, by deposition from office, by certain ecclesiastical censures and vindicative penalties.[75] Note that the canon speaks of the complete loss of power in the delegator. Hence the statement by Maroto that the suspension of the power of the

[72] C. 19, X, *eo. tit.*, I, 29; Jaffé, n. 15443; c. 20, X, *eo. tit.*, I, 29; Jaffé, n. 15751; c. 30, X, *eo. tit.*, I, 29; Jaffé, n. 3664.

[73] Canon 207, § 1—"Potestas delegata extinguitur . . . non autem resoluto iure delegantis, nisi in duobus casibus de quibus in can. 61." The exceptions referred to in canon 61 appear as follows: ". . . nisi aliud ex additis clausulis appareat, aut rescriptum contineat potestatem alicui factam concedendi gratiam peculiaribus personis in eodem expressis, et res adhuc integra sit."

[74] Kearney, p. 115; Naz, I, n. 494, 3°; Wernz-Vidal, II, n. 377, 6°; Ayrinhac, *General Legislation*, p. 376.

[75] Michiels, II, 473-474; Maroto, I, n. 713, I.

delegator produces the same effect, *res adhuc integra,* on the power of the delegate is devoid of legal basis.[76] Since delegated power ordinarily does not cease even upon the complete cessation of the right of the delegator, how much less will it cease, therefore, as the effect of a suspension?[77]

The first exception to the continued efficacy of delegated power is stated thus: *nisi aliud ex additis clausulis appareat.* This clause means that delegated power continues unless, from the formulas used in the rescript of delegation, it can be demonstrated conclusively that the delegation has not been given absolutely but conditionally or dependently on the will of the delegator.[78] Such a clause is exemplified in the phrase *"ad beneplacitum nostrum"* or in equivalent phrases.[79] The customary equivalent phrases adduced by authors are: *"ad suae voluntatis beneplacitum," "donec voluero," "donec mihi placuerit," "durante meo munere," "donec vixero,"* or *"pro temore nostrae voluntatis."*[80] These phrases when inserted in the rescript bring about the extinction of power in the delegate because, as O'Neill (1900-1943) adroitly observed, they presuppose the perseverance of the delegator in his original will, which ceases with him, so that, having lost his right, he can no longer juridically will or please or displease.[81]

Some phrases are commonly admitted as insufficient to affect the continuance of the delegated power. Thus the phrase *"ad beneplacitum Sedis"* leaves the power of a delegate undisturbed, for the *Sedes* itself does not die with the decease of its incumbent. Delegation made with this phrase is perpetual and will endure until affected by one of the

[76] Maroto, I, n. 716.

[77] Chelodi, n. 129, e; Coronata, I, n. 290, 6°; Kearney, p. 116.

[78] Maroto, I, n. 713, I, 1°; Wernz-Vidal, II, n. 377, 6°; Roberti, I, n. 141, V.

[79] Canons 73; 183, § 2.

[80] Toso, Lib. II, Tom. I, p. 176; Regatillo, *Ius Sacram.*, n. 437, g; Roberti, I, n. 141, V; O'Neill, p. 199; Coronata, I, n. 290, 6°.

[81] O'Neill, p. 199; Van Hove, *De Rescr.*, n. 296; Toso, Lib. II, Tom. I, p. 176; Michiels, II, 474.

other causes effecting the cessation of delegated power.[82]

The phrases "*usque ad revocationem,*" "*donec revocavero,*" or "*donec aliter ordinavero,*" do not abrogate delegated power when the grantor dies. In order to touch or affect delegated power, these phrases postulate a positive contrary act by which the concession is revoked. Now such an act cannot be elicited after the dissolution of the delegator's right nor is the very dissolution of his right such an act. For these reasons it must be concluded that the delegated power will remain unchanged upon the death of the grantor, unless, of course, antecedently to his death the contrary will was manifested.[83]

If a clause relative to a temporal limitation of the delegation is expressed in the rescript, the power ceases when that determined time has elapsed.[84] Van Hove (1872-1947) correctly pointed out that when a personal *beneplacitum* clause together with a clause relative to a predetermined period of time is used in the same rescript, the delegation remains even after the death of the delegator, if the period of time has not elapsed.[85]

Should it happen that the meaning of some clause or phrase is not clear, Maroto (1875-1937) advanced a safe norm to follow. He stated that, in doubt, when the delegation seems to follow from the special benignity of the grantor, it must be considered equivalent to being given *donec revocavero* or *ad beneplacitum Sedis,* and therefore does not cease with the death of the delegator; when the delegation appears to be granted as a burden (*pro munere*), it is to be inferred as being given *ad beneplacitum nostrum.*[86] Note always that the legislator requires that such

[82] Michiels, II, 475; O'Neill, p. 199.

[83] Van Hove, *De Rescr.*, n. 296; Michiels, II, 475; Maroto, I, n. 713, I, 1°.

[84] Cf. *supra*, pp. 42-48. Exception, of course, is made for acts of the internal forum placed through inadvertence.—Can. 207, § 2.

[85] Van Hove, *De Rescr.*, n. 297.

[86] Maroto, I, n. 713, I, 1°.

a clause or phrase be evident; hence the clause or phrase is never presumed.[87]

Relative to the phrase *ad beneplacitum nostrum* or its equivalent, it is disputed whether delegated power ceases with the death of the grantor only when the commission is still integral and intact (*re adhuc integra*), or whether it ceases also when the use of the delegated power has been set in motion. The dispute is not centered upon the presence or absence of a clause or phrase pointing to a *res adhuc aut non amplius integra.* Without a doubt such a clause or phrase could be inserted, but on the supposition that only the phrase *ad beneplacitum nostrum* or its equivalent is stated, how is the cessation of delegated power to be judged? Maroto argued that, if the delegate has already undertaken to execute his commission, the jurisdiction has become firmly established in him and will remain uneffected by the death of the grantor, despite the *beneplacitum* clause.[88] Michiels argues for the verity of this opinion on the basis that good order demands the uninterruption of what is already begun.[89] Kearney simply says that if the mandate so provides, the delegation will end with the death, civil or natural, of the delegator, unless the matter is no longer intact.[90]

According to the obvious meaning of the phrase *ad beneplacitum nostrum,* the assertion which states that delegated power ends regardless of the status of the matter, is preferred. This or any equivalent phrase postulates the continued existence of the will of the grantor, and the power is dependent upon that will, as is readily admitted by Maroto and Michiels, although they hold the contrary opinion.[91] Through physical or juridical death, that positive supporting will is extinguished, and hence the foundation for the dele-

[87] Reg. 15, R. J., in VI°; Roelker, p. 120.
[88] Maroto, I, n. 713, I, 1°.
[89] Michiels, II, 475.
[90] Kearney, pp. 115-116.
[91] Maroto, I, n. 713, I, 1°; Michiels, II, 474.

gated power is removed. This phrase, therefore, acts as an antecedent revocatory will already intimated.

To maintain that a delegated power does not cease simply on the basis that a delegated power is rendered firm and permanent through its use, goes beyond the meaning of the phrase, and, in the opinion of others, the writer not excluded, it goes beyond the restrictive terminology of canon 207, § 1.[92] The assertion by Michiels that good order demands the uninterruption of what is already begun can properly be countered. As a general principle the assertion is admissible, but its verification here rests upon the supposistion that *de facto* the uninterruption is essential to good order in this case. That which depends upon the will of the grantor but still circumvents that will cannot be identified with good order.

The whole crux of this dispute rests squarely on whether the word *"et"* in canon 61 is to be taken disjunctively so as to refer also to the first part of the *nisi* clause, or whether it is to be taken conjunctively only with reference to the second part of the *nisi* clause.[93] Because of the dispute, since the present law is a restatement of the old, one must revert to the pre-Code jurisprudence. The argument from the earlier law conclusively favors the second opinion, which has been the long-standing discipline of the Church

[92] Van Hove, *De Rescr.*, n. 295; O'Neill, p. 201. By their division of the matter, the following authors concur with this opinion. Cf. Wernz-Vidal, II, n. 377, 6°; Blat, II, n. 156; Ramstein, p. 167; Brys, I, n. 376, I, 6°; Toso, Lib. II, Tom. I, p. 176; Naz, I, n. 494, 3°; Prümmer, p. 122; Badii, I, n. 148; Vermeersch-Creusen, I, n. 322, 5°; Regatillo, *Ius Sacram.*, n. 437, g; Coronata, I, n. 290, 6°; Bouuaert-Simenon, I, n. 361; Woywod, *A Practical Commentary on the Code of Canon Law* (2 vols., 8. printing, revised by C. Smith, New York: Joseph F. Wagner—London: B. Herder, 1944), I, p. 45 (hereafter cited Woywod); Chelodi, n. 81, c.

[93] Canon 61—"...nullum... rescriptum perimitur, nisi aliud ex additis clausulis appareat, aut rescriptum contineat potestatem alicui factam concedendi gratiam peculiaribus personis in eodem expressis, et res adhuc integra sit."

based upon c. 5, *de rescriptis,* I, 3, in VI°.[94] As a corroboratory observation, the non-applicability of the clause, *et res adhuc integra sit,* to the first part of the *nisi* clause is further enhanced by the *Schema* for these canons (61 and 207, § 1), wherein no mention is made of the clause, *et res adhuc integra sit,* in relation to this exception.[95]

The second exception of canon 61 as made applicable through canon 207, § 1, declares that delegated power does not cease *resoluto iure delegantis* unless the delegation grants the power of conceding a favor to the persons determined in the rescript and the concession of power is still unused when the power of the delegator ceases.[96] Therefore in order to affect delegated power, this second exception postulates two things: firstly, the delegation must contain what is called a *gratia facienda,* and secondly, the matter must still be integral when the grantor loses his right.

In order to constitute a *gratia facienda,* the immediate object of the delegation is the power or the faculty which actually is to be exercised in favor of a person or persons expressly determined in the rescript. These conditions are fulfilled in a rescript granted *in forma commissoria* with a voluntary executor in which those to be favored are specifically designated. Thus a *gratia facienda* merely refers to a rescript in which the favor is actually to be granted by the executor himself in virtue of power received from the grantor, whereas the expression *gratia facta* means that the favor has already been granted by the one who issued the rescript and the executor merely applies the favor to the parties.[97]

[94] Van Hove, *De Rescr.,* n. 295; O'Neill, p. 198.

[95] Cf. *Schema C. I. C.,* Lib. II, can. 111, § 1; Lib. I, can 63; Lib. III, can. 152, § 2.

[96] Canon 207, § 1—"Potestas delegata extinguitur... non autem resoluto iure delegantis, nisi... [canon 61]... rescriptum contineat potestatem alicui factam concedendi gratiam peculiaribus personis in eodem expressis, et res adhuc integra sit."

[97] O'Neill, p. 199; Coronata, I, n. 82, 3°.

Michiels cites the following example. The power is given to Peter, a priest, for dispensing from a matrimonial impediment of crime between Paul and Mary. In such a commission the favor is not already granted to the parties (*gratia facta*) by the delegator, but rather is to be granted or denied by the delegate, who is constituted as a true delegate.[98] Hence, so long as the condition, *et res adhuc integra sit,* obtains, the favor is truly a *gratia facienda,* and no right has been acquired by the designated persons, much less by the delegate, since the favor is not intended for him.[99] Hence, *si res adhuc integra sit,* the delegated power ends when the delegator's right or power is dissolved. Of course, even if the matter had been undertaken, a delegation of this kind would cease *resoluto iure delegantis* if there was also appended the phrase *"ad beneplacitum nostrum,"* or some equivalent.[100]

By way of exclusion, delegated power does not cease, *re adhuc integra,* when the rescript is granted *in forma commissoria* with a voluntary executor and the beneficiaries are not specified in the rescript, e.g., the faculty granted to some priest for absolving from reserved cases or of dispensing certain matrimonial impediments, as well as the faculty to grant a favor for a certain number of cases or a determined time or to a certain community.[101] This kind of delegation, of course, supposing the absence of a personal *beneplacitum* phrase, would not cease *resoluto iure delegantis,* because it is considered to be not a *gratia facienda,* but rather a *gratia facta,* since, as in the examples cited, the priest is truly the beneficiary of the rescript.[102] Hence in effect it is a delegation made *in forma gratiosa,* since the object of the delegation is the favor which is granted directly and immediately to the delegate, rather than to a third person, even though in the exercise of the power

[98] Michiels, II, 476.

[99] O'Neill, p. 200.

[100] O'Neill, p. 201; Chelodi, n. 81, c.

[101] Michiels, II, 476-477; Coronata, I, n. 82, in nota 5, p. 92.

[102] Michiels, *loc. cit.;* Maroto, I, n. 713, I, 2, b; O'Neill, p. 200.

that has been conferred a benefit will redound to a third party.[103]

Also excluded is a rescript given *in forma commissoria* with a necessary executor. The power of this executor is not precisely that of conceding the favor, since he merely applies the favor which was already granted by the grantor of the rescript. This executor must investigate the truth of the petition, but is not free to deny the favor except in the three instances enumerated in canon 54, § 1.[104] The party to receive the favor has a *ius ad rem*; the favor itself is a *gratia facta*. Therefore, unless there is a clause to the contrary, this kind of executory power follows the general rule and does not cease *resoluto iure rescribentis*.[105]

The second condition which must be verified for the cessation of the delegated power of a voluntary executor for conferring a favor on expressly mentioned persons is this, that the delegate has undertaken the matter before the death occurred. In matters of voluntary jurisdiction the matter is considered to be no longer intact if the executor has begun to execute his mandate.[106] If it is a matter that pertains to the sacramental forum, the matter is no longer integral when the delegate begins to hear the confession of the person expressly referred to in the rescript.[107] Hence, should it happen that absolution is delayed, the death of the delegator would not affect the power of the delegate.[108] In the extra-sacramental forum or the external forum, the matter is undertaken when the executor begins to inquire about the truthfulness of the petition, e.g., by sending out a list of questions to be proposed to the party or to witnesses.[109] It is disputed whether simply the judg-

[103] Bouuaert-Simenon, I, n. 361.

[104] O'Neill, pp. 169-170.

[105] Van Hove, *De Rescr.*, n. 301; Michiels, II, 476.

[106] Van Hove, *De Rescr.*, n. 304; Coronata, I, n. 82, 4°; Maroto, I, n. 713, I, 2°.

[107] Maroto, *loc. cit.;* Van Hove, *De Rescr.*, n. 304.

[108] Maroto, I, n. 713, I, 2°, in nota 1.

[109] Van Hove, *De Rescr.*, n. 304; Coronata, I, n. 82, 4°; Michiels, II, 477.

ment concerning the integrity and authenticity of the rescript suffices to disrupt the integralness of the matter. The better opinion seems to be the affirmative one.[110] It is generally held that the mere designation of a substitute by the executor still leaves the matter integral.[111] Also invalid acts would not disrupt the integralness of the matter.[112]

According to Decretal Law relative to judicial jurisdiction, it was sharply disputed when a matter ceased to be intact. From a letter of Lucius III (1181-1185) it was argued that the matter was no longer integral when the *litis contestatio* had occurred.[113] Urban III (1185-1187) said the matter was undertaken when the citation was made.[114] The constant opinion even from the time of the earliest decretalists has conformed to the letter of Urban III[115] This common teaching is embodied in the Code in canon 1725, 1°, which clearly states that the matter is no longer integral once the citation has legitimately been made or when the parties spontaneously appear in court.

An analysis of the terminology in canon 61 has prompted the question whether rescripts of justice are within the purview of the provisions of canon 207, § 1, relative to the consideration of the words *resoluto iure delegantis.* Contrary to the earlier law, which stated that rescripts of justice expire, *re adhuc integra,* with the death of the grantor, the general rule of canon 207, § 1 is applied to rescripts of justice because no distinction is made in that

[110] O'Neill, p. 201; Coronata, I, n. 82, 4°; Michiels, II, 477.

[111] Van Hove, *De Rescr.*, n. 304; Michiels, II, 477.

[112] O'Neill, pp. 201-202; Van Hove, *De Rescr.*, n. 304, in nota 4.

[113] C. 19, X, *de officio et potestate iudicis delegati,* I, 29; Jaffé, n. 15443.

[114] C. 20, X, *eo. tit.*, I, 29; Jaffé, n. 15751. Cf. also c. 10, X, *de officio legati,* I, 30; Potthast, n. 9561; c. 19, X, *de foro competenti,* II, 2; Potthast, n. 9586.

[115] Cf. Panormitanus, lib. I, tit. XXIX, c. XIX, n. 6; Pirhing, lib. I, tit. XXIX, n. 176; Sanchez, lib. VIII, disp. XXVIII, n. 13; Ferraris, s. v. *delegare,* nn. 45-53; Wernz, II, n. 561, V.

canon.[116] Moreover canon 1606 brings delegated judges directly under the principles of canon 207. Wherefore the statement by Coronata that rescripts of justice never come under the provisions of canon 207, § 1, seems much too broad, and the statement that the exception refers only to rescripts of favor appears obviously untenable.[117]

The application of the provision of canon 207, § 1, regulating the cessation of rescripts of justice, is evident when it is made to the first exception stated in canon 61, namely, *nisi aliud ex additis clausulis appareat.* It is beyond question that the *beneplacitum nostrum* phrase or its equivalent may be inserted in the rescript of judicial delegation. When such phrases are clearly evident, the power of the delegated judge ceases *resoluto iure delegantis.*[118]

Can it also be admitted that a rescript of justice is included in the second exception of canon 61 as applied through canon 207, § 1? Some authors place a rescript of justice under the second exception because, as they say, sometimes the rescript of justice contains a favor.[119] Others maintain that rescripts of justice come under the general rule of canon 207, § 1, and also under the first exception, not however under the second exception. Thus, e.g., Van Hove (1872-1947) maintained that the delegated power of a judge for hearing a case does not cease with the death of the delegator, even though the delegate has not issued the citation when the demise occurred, unless a clause to the contrary is inserted in the rescript.[120] The non-applicability of the second exception to rescripts of justice is rightly maintained, because such a rescript does not contain the power of conferring a favor (*gratia*) on determined persons mentioned in the rescript.[121]

[116] Van Hove, *De Rescr.*, n. 303; Michiels, II, 475, in nota 3; Toso, Lib. I, 145.

[117] Coronata, I, n. 82, 1°.

[118] Van Hove, *De Rescr.*, n. 304; and in nota 2, p. 276.

[119] Michiels, II, 475, in nota 3; Chelodi, n. 81, in nota 4, p. 136.

[120] Van Hove, *De Rescr.*, n. 303.

[121] Van Hove, *loc. cit.;* Toso, Lib. I, 146; Coronata, I, n. 82, 1°.

To the two exceptions referred to by canon 207, § 1 in the text of canon 61, Kearney maintains that a third must be added. Adverting to the words of canon 1725, 3°, which declares that, when the legitimate citation or its equivalent has taken place, the jurisdiction of a delegated judge is endowed with firmness, so that it does not expire by the death of the delegator,[122] he concludes that, before the citation or its equivalent has occurred, the delegated judicial power ends with the termination of the right of the superior. By appealing to the earlier law, he summarizes his opinion by saying that it is in keeping with that law to include this third exception, and it is, he maintains, in harmony with the new law, since otherwise canon 1725, 3°, would be without meaning.[123] Concerning this opinion, no one would dispute that it is in keeping with the pre-Code legislation. However, that it is in harmony with the Code is not shown by Kearney.

Canon 1606 expressly places delegated judges under the provisions of canon 207, § 1, and cites no exceptions.[124] Canon 207, § 1 provides for the non-cessation of delegated power except in two cases, namely, when a clause to the contrary is clearly evident in the rescript of delegation, and when the power granted concerns a *gratia facienda* (i.e., establishes the delegate as a voluntary executor for granting a favor to persons expressly designated in the rescript) and the delegate has not begun to exercise his commission.

The sequence of canon 1725, 3° is this, that the citation makes delegated power firm so that it does not cease *resoluto iure delegantis*. To say, therefore, that the lack of citation or its equivalent with reference to the words *resoluto iure delegantis* extinguishes delegated power seems

[122] Canon 1725—"Cum citatio legitima peracta fuerit aut partes sponte in iudicium venerint... 3°. In iudice delegato firma redditur iurisdictio ita ut non expiret resoluto iure delegantis."

[123] Kearney, p. 116. This opinion is also held by Lega-Bartoccetti (I, p. 203) and Roberti (I, n. 141, V).

[124] Canon 1606—"Delegati iudices servare tenentur regulas statutas in can. 199-207, 209."

logical enough. But on what basis is this alleged effect, namely the cessation of delegated power, founded? Certainly not on the general principle of canon 207, § 1, contained in the words *resoluto iure delegantis,* because this principle argues for the continued existence of the power. The factual statement of canon 1725, 3° is in agreement with this general principle; the conclusion drawn by Kearney is opposed. Furthermore, the basis is certainly not found in the first exception given in the law of canon 61, for in canon 1725, 3°, there is no question of a personal *beneplacitum.*

Can a legal basis for the conclusion which Kearney draws from canon 1725, 3°, be found in the second exception to the general rule of canon 207, § 1? This second exception does not directly encompass the situation envisioned in canon 1725, 3°, for it seems highly improbable that the power of a delegated judge is to be considered as a *gratia facienda.* A judicial sentence is a matter of justice. Only by the broadest analogy could the power of a judge delegated to hear a controversy between designated persons, and to give a sentence in favor of one of the parties, come under the notion of a favor (*gratia*). This very broad similarity seems to be the only means of bringing the conclusion drawn from canon 1725, 3°, into conformity with the principles of canon 207, § 1 that relate to the words *resoluto iure delegantis.*

The reluctance to admit canon 1725, 3° as the basis for a third exception to canon 207, § 1 rests on several points, the first being the express subjection of delegated judges to the norms of canon 207, § 1. This statement of canon 1606 is clear and definite. Secondly, such an exception departs from the clearly restrictive terms of canon 207, § 1 (found in canon 61), relative to the consideration of the words *resoluto iure delegantis.* To appeal to the pre-Code teaching is to go beyond the terms of the present law, clearly determined in canon 207, § 1, and would create the very discord which the opinion of Kearney supposes to exist and desires to amend. By way of conclusion, therefore, it is proposed that the clause, "*ita ut non expiret* [*potestas iudicis*] *resoluto iure delegantis*" of canon 1725, 3°, be classified as a mere expletive statement of fact, without the inference that, if the citation has not been issued, *resoluto iure delegantis,* the power of the judge no longer endures.[125]

This proposal is in accordance with the provisions of canon 207, § 1, which provisions receive a strict interpretation in this matter (a *rescriptum ad lites*) according to canon 50. If the inference of Kearney is insisted upon, then canon 207, § 1 has application by way of analogy inasmuch as, and if, the delegatory rescript *ad lites* is to be considered as a favor to the parties in the terms of canon 61. However, while the rescript *ad lites* may be a favor, this canon speaks of an execution of a rescript in favor of certain parties. The execution of a rescript *ad lites* is never a favor to the parties. Its execution is the impartial conduct of a judicial trial with the awarding of the decision to one of the parties in justice.

[125] Van Hove (*De Rescr.*, n. 304, in nota 3, p. 277) in conjunction with the last remarks in n. 303 certainly seems to imply this conclusion; also Coronata, I, n. 82, 1°, who expressly states that the earlier law has been changed.

CHAPTER V

CESSATION BY REASON OF THE PERSON DELEGATED

Besides the extinction of delegated power by reason of some intrinsic condition or by reason of the extrinsic cause, its cessation may also be effected by some act or condition on the part of the passive subject of delegated power. Of course, it is presupposed that this passive subject or the delegate has been validly and licitly constituted in the position of a delegate.

Under Title V, *De potestate ordinaria et delegata,* the legislator has not described the personal qualifications required for the office of a delegate. Pre-Code jurisprudence utilized the following verse to express these qualities.

> Liber, mas, gnarus, cui sit mens, integra fama,
> Aetas, qui subsit; committitur huic bene causa.[1]

For the present law, the following general principle may be adduced. All who are not excluded either by nature or by law, and who are endowed with the required qualifications, can become the bearers of a delegation or a subdelegation.[2]

One who lacks the use of reason is, by nature, incapable (*incapax*) of validly receiving delegation; by divine law, an infidel is likewise *incapax.*[3] According to ecclesiastical law, one who is not a cleric cannot validly obtain delegated jurisdiction except from the Holy See.[4] Also by law the *delegandus* must not be subject to an ecclesiastical censure, which in some cases renders not only the acquisition, but also the retention of power, sometimes

[1] Cf. Hostiensis, lib. I, *de officio et potestate iudicis delegati,* n. 3; Ferraris, s. v. *delegare,* n. 25.

[2] Brys, I, n. 369, II; Maroto, I, n. 708.

[3] Regatillo, I, n. 358; Maroto, I, n. 708. It is disputed whether women are prohibited by divine law. Maroto (*loc. cit.*) maintains the affirmative "*probabiliter.*"

[4] Canon 118. Cf. Maroto, *loc. cit.*

invalid and sometimes illicit.[5] In other instances the law has established certain enactments that are to be followed when power is delegated to another.[6] Concerning the requisite qualifications, the delegate must be both worthy and juridically suitable in proportion to the gravity of the matter delegated. Concerning the confessors for women religious, e.g., the Code has determined these qualities.[7]

The passive subject of delegation may be a subject or a non-subject of the delegator, for, as Maroto (1875-1937) stated, delegation is a favor which can be conferred even upon one not subject to the delegator.[8] This difference, however, is noteworthy. The non-subject cannot be forced to accept the delegation, whereas a passive subject who is under the jurisdictional authority of the grantor can be obliged to receive the delegation or subdelegation. Maroto here used the word *"acceptandi"* and then proceeded to state that an express or tacit acceptance on the part of the delegate is required.[9]

Nevertheless the question concerning the necessity of acceptance has always been sharply disputed. Prior to the Code the more common opinion demanded the necessity of acceptance even for validity, since delegation was looked upon as a sort of *donatio,* which had effect only upon acceptance.[10] This dispute has continued even under the Code, although the former negative opinion is becoming the more common. Kearney summarizes the question and arrives at a sound conclusion. He rightly says that the Code has given more weight to the former less common opinion, and inasmuch as a *dubium iuris* exists it is to be

[5] Cf. canons 2258, § 2; 2264; 2265; 2266; 2275, 3°; 2283; 2284; 2314, § 1. Cf. Maroto, I, n. 576, D-E.

[6] Cf. canons 874; 875; 1096; 1573, § 4; 1607.

[7] Canon 524, § 1.

[8] Maroto, I, n. 709, 2ª.

[9] Maroto, *loc. cit.* Cf. also Coronata, I, n. 289; Brys, I, n. 370, II.

[10] Oesterle, *Consultationes de Jure Matrimoniali* (Romae: Officium Libri Catholici, 1942), p. 341 (hereafter cited *Consultationes*); Kearney, pp. 92-93.

concluded in virtue of canon 15 that an acceptance is not required for validity.[11]

The present chapter considers this passive subject of delegation in his relation to the cessation of delegated power. Although the Code in canon 207, § 1 has for the cessation of delegated power expressly enumerated only one cause as arising on the part of the delegate, namely, renunciation, this chapter contains two articles because, as will be obvious, the specification of the Code is not exclusive. Attention is first given to renunciation, then to the extinction of the power of the delegate through a natural or a legal death (*resoluto iure delegati*).

ARTICLE 1. *Renuntiatione Delegati*

The provisions of the Code of Canon Law relative to the cessation of delegated power by reason of renunciation are precise and explicit. Canon 207, § 1 states that delegated power is extinguished by renunciation on the part of the delegate, which renunciation must be directly intimated to and accepted by the grantor.[12]

Section I. Historical Note

Concerning the renunciation of delegated power, there is no explicit citation to be found in Book I, Title 29, *de officio et potestate iudicis delegati,* of the Decretals of Gregory IX (1227-1241), or in the similar title found in the Decretals of Boniface VIII (1294-1303) and Clement V (1305-1314). Perhaps this omission may be explained by the fact that Decretal Law had a Title, *De renunciatione,*[13] which directly pertained to the renunciation of ecclesiastical offices and benefices.

[11] Kearney, p. 94; Oesterle, *Consultationes,* pp. 337-347. Cf. also Galassi, "De delegatione ad matrimonio assistendum," *Ephemerides Iuris Canonici,* II (1946), 347-352; "S. R. Rota Sententiae Recentiores," *Ephemerides Iuris Canonici, loc. cit.*

[12] Canon 207, § 1—"Potestas delegata extinguitur ... renuntiatione delegati deleganti directe intimata et ab eodem acceptata; ...."

[13] X, *de renunciatione,* I, 9; *eo. tit.,* I, 7, in VI°; *eo. tit.,* I, 4, in Clem.

Whether this latter title was extended to substantiate the cessation of delegated power is difficult to determine. Renunciation was defined as the spontaneous and free remission of one's own right, [14] and in this broad sense it could seem applicable to the renunciation of delegated power. Whether, in fact, this application was made seems doubtful, particularly in view of the general silence of even outstanding canonists. Thus Reiffenstuel (1642-1703)[15] and Schmalzgrueber (1663-1735)[16] made no mention of renunciation among the causes extinguishing delegated power; moreover, the few references made to the renunciation of delegated power did not appeal to the Title, *De renunciatione.*

However, that the renunciation of delegated power was an institute of pre-Code jurisprudence may be sustained because of several references to it among commentators. Only two references were found in the *Glossa Ordinaria* under the Title, *De officio et potestate iudicis delegati.* The one merely mentioned the renunciation of power without any further pertinent qualifications;[17] the second stated a presumption of law that one had renounced his right when he acted contrary to it.[18] The direct application of these statements to the cessation of delegated power, however, is not clear. Gonzalez-Tellez (fl. 1673) spoke of resignation in favor of a third party.[19] Pirhing (1606-1679), on the other hand, referred to a delegated judge

[14] Hostiensis, lib. I, *de renunciatione,* n. 1; Pichler, lib. I, tit. IX, n. 1; Pirhing, lib. I, tit. IX, n. 1.

[15] Reiffenstuel, lib. I, tit. XXIX, nn. 125-154.

[16] Schmalzgrueber, lib. I, tit. XXIX, nn. 40-50.

[17] *Glossa Ordinaria* ad c. 12, X, *de officio et potestate iudicis delegati,* I, 29, s. v. *Dimittere.*

[18] *Glossa Ordinaria* ad c. 20, X, *eo. tit.,* I, 29, s. v. *Recessum.*

[19] Gonzalez-Tellez, lib. I, tit. XXIX, c. XII, n. 4. McDevitt notes that prior to the Code this was a special kind of renunciation. Cf. *The Renunciation of an Ecclesiastical Office,* The Catholic University of America Canon Law Studies, n. 218 (Washington, D. C.: The Catholic University of America Press, 1946), p. 8 (hereafter cited McDevitt).

renouncing delegation given *intuitu dignitatis suae.*[20] Later, Ferraris († ca. 1763) simply reproduced the words of Pirhing, while Wernz (1842-1914) spoke of the resignation of a delegated judge legitimately made.[21]

Of all the pre-Code commentators, perhaps D'Annibale 1815-1892) made the most direct statement when he taught that renunciation on the part of the delegate, if it was directly intimated, extinguished the delegated power.[22] As the legal basis for this proposition, he appealed to the Rule of Roman Law (D. (50. 17) 35) which was expressed anew in Rule 1 of the Rules of Law of Gregory IX.[23] This appeal was founded on the more common opinion prior to the Code that acceptance of the delegated power by the delegate was necessary.[24] According to the law of the Code, this requirement seems no longer to stand.[25]

Section II. Canonical Commentary

Even though the precise historical basis for the cessation of delegated power because of renunciation may not be evident, it is clearly a legal institute of the Code of Canon Law. The Code designates renunciation as the sixth reason for the cessation of delegated power. But the mere renunciation itself is insufficient, since canon 207, § 1 expressly attaches to this active surrender two subsequent

[20] Pirhing, lib. I, tit. XXIX, n. 175. From the context of this statement it appears that the dignity itself was renounced, and only as a consequence was the delegated power lost.

[21] Ferraris, s. v. *delegare,* n. 54, 4°; Wernz, II, n. 561, VI. Here Wernz in dealing with the question of resignation cited c. 21, § 1, X, *de officio et potestate iudicis delegati,* I, 29. In this place, however, renunciation is not expressly stated, although it could be inferred.

[22] D'Annibale, I, n. 77, 3°.

[23] C. 1, X, *de regulis iuris,* V, 41—"Omnis res, per quascunque causas nascitur, per easdem dissolvitur."

[24] D'Annibale, I, n. 74, 3°. For a detailed treatment of this disputed opinion cf. Van Hove, *De Rescr.,* nn. 113-118; Michiels, II, 320-323; O'Neill, pp. 84-86.

[25] Canon 37. Cf. Van Hove, *De Rescr.,* nn. 119, 123. Hence Coronata (I, n. 290, 5°) wrongly appeals to the Rules of Law just mentioned.

acts that are absolutely necessary before any effect is had on the renounced delegated power. These two requisites are direct intimation and acceptance.[26] Hence as a cause affecting the continuance of a delegated power, renunciation may be considered from the viewpoint of the one eliciting and manifesting the renunciatory will, and from the viewpoint of the one who renders that renunciatory will efficacious by acceptance. The first may be considered as renunciation *in actu primo;* the latter, as renunciation *in actu secundo.* Renunciation as a cause effecting the cessation of delegated power will be a combination of these two, each of which alone is insufficient.

An analysis of renunciation *in actu primo* gives rise to four considerations, namely: 1) the capacity to elicit the renunciatory will, 2) the act itself, 3) the authorization or competence to place such an act, and 4) the official manifestation of the renunciatory will to the delegator. These four are treated successively.

1. In the first place the capacity of renouncing delegated power is considered as the fundamental or natural ability of placing the act of renunciation. At first glance it is evident that the act of renunciation, being a human act, can be elicited only by those who possess the use of their rational faculties. Should the use of these faculties be lost permanently, then by the natural law itself an act of renunciation is impossible. In the event that the loss is merely temporary, for the same reason the act could not occur during that time. Moreover, by reason of the necessity of knowledge and volition, a renunciatory act placed because of extrinsic force which cannot be resisted is considered as not having been placed.[27] Grave fear brought about even unjustly and also deceit would not render the

[26] Canon 207, § 1—"Potestas delegata extinguitur . . . renuntiatione delegati deleganti directe intimata et ab eodem acceptata; . . . ."

[27] Canon 103, § 1. By way of analogy to the renunciation of an ecclesiastical office cf. McDevitt, pp. 92-93.

renunciatory will void unless the law ruled otherwise.[28] Nevertheless in such a case, either at the instance of the injured party or *ex officio,* the act can be subjected to rescission through the sentence of a judge.[29] Even error, if of course it be substantial or amount to a *conditio sine qua non,* annuls a renunciatory act.[30]

2. Having mentioned these conditions as affecting the eliciting of the act of renunciation, one may next consider the act itself. Although contrary to its usual practice the Code has not defined the term in question, here renunciation in itself may be defined as a human act by which is indicated the will of dismissing or handing back what has been received from another. Or, analogously to the renunciation of privileges and the renunciation of an ecclesiastical office, it may be designated as the voluntary resignation or cession of delegated power.[31] The act of renunciation, therefore, intends to touch the power itself; it is not the mere non-use of the delegated jurisdiction.[32]

Since canon 207, § 1 neither attaches any exception to the statement on renunciation nor appends any qualifying expression to the word *renuntiatione,* it is valid to conclude in the first place that any act of the will which indicates the renunciatory intent of the delegate is sufficient to constitute an act of renunciation. The renunciatory intent, therefore, may be express, as when in writing or orally, clear and formal words are expressly used, or it may be tacit, as when the renunciatory will is not expressly manifested, but is deducible from other facts, or also from acts to the contrary.[33] Renunciation may, moreover, be ab-

[28] Canon 103, § 2. By way of analogy to the renunciation of an ecclesiastical office cf. McDevitt, pp. 93-97.

[29] Canon 103, § 2; also canons 1684-1689.

[30] Canon 104. Cf. McDevitt, pp. 97-98.

[31] Regatillo, I, n. 346; Michiels, II, 613; Van Hove, *De Priv.-De Disp.,* n. 236, in proem.

[32] Cf. canons 37; 69; 76. Cf. also Roelker, pp. 108-109; Michiels, II, 613.

[33] Michiels, II, 613; Van Hove, *De Rescr.,* n. 236, in proem.

solute or conditional, depending on whether the expressed renunciatory intent in unqualified by any condition or whether it is restricted through some proviso.[34]

3. The second conclusion from the unrestricted statement of canon 207, § 1 provides an answer to the following question. Who is competent to place an act of renunciation? By this is meant, does the Code exclude or restrict any delegate from exercising the radical capacity of placing an act of renunciation? Note that it is not the natural capacity of renouncing that is considered here; a renunciatory act can be effected by any free agent. Here is considered only the legal competence (in the sense of no prohibition) of renouncing.

Inasmuch as the law in canon 207, § 1 uses the most general term without any restriction, *scil., renuntiatione delegati,* it is concluded that every kind of delegated power can be subjected to the renunciatory will of the possessor. Were any particular kind of delegated jurisdiction to be excluded, the legislator could have easily made provision for this by the insertion of a clause to that effect. No such provision is found either in canon 207, § 1, or in the other canons of Title V. Hence, whether the delegated power was derived *ab homine* or *a iure,*[35] or was granted *ad universitatem causarum* or *in singulis casibus,* that delegated power comes under the renunciatory will of the delegate.[36] Note well, however, that although the renunciatory intent can be elicited and manifested, the efficacious renunciation is not accomplished by this alone.

An objection may be raised relative to habitual faculties. These are considered as *privilegia praeter ius*[37] and, it

[34] Cf. McDevitt, p. 9.

[35] Cappello (*Summa,* I, n. 258, 5°, in nota 11) states that the renunciation is restricted to a delegation deriving *ab homine.*

[36] This opinion seems to be sustained by a negative argument. Among the commentators on the Code it was found that Cappello, just cited, was the only author to advance any restriction. All others in their treatment of Title V are silent.

[37] Canon 66, § 1.

would seem, are therefore governed by the principles given in the Title V, *De Privilegiis.* Canon 72, § 1 states that privileges cease through renunciation accepted by the competent superior.[38] In the same canon it is stated that private persons may not renounce privileges granted to a dignity.[39] The question, therefore, arises: will the habitual faculties, e.g., the Quinquennial Faculties of local ordinaries, be governed by the unrestricted provisions of canon 207, § 1, or will canon 72, § 3, also come into play?

First of all, the Quinquennial Faculties are not merely viewed as privileges *praeter ius,* but are definitely considered as delegated power.[40] Therefore their cessation will be governed conjointly by canon 207, § 1 and at least canon 72, § 1. Whether canon 73, § 3 is applicable depends on the nature of the faculty to be renounced. Those faculties that are personal privileges may be renounced on the strength of canon 207, § 1, and canon 72, §§ 1-2.[41] However, even those faculties that contain real privileges or privileges to be used in favor of one's subjects or territory, can be validly renounced *in actu primo,* although they may not be licitly so renounced. The fact that there is question simply of illicitness seems to be based on the

[38] Canon 72, § 1—"Privilegia cessant per renuntiationem a competente Superiore acceptatam."

[39] Canon 72, § 3—"Concesso alicui communitati, dignitati locove renuntiare privatis personis non licet." It is disputed whether '*non licet*' has also an invalidating effect. Michiels (II, 617, in nota 2) holds the affirmative, since *ex rerum natura* there is required a *habilitas renunciandi,* which he supposes to be lacking in matters of real privileges. Van Hove (*De Priv.-De Disp.,* n. 244), with greater probability, holds the negative, since the act of renunciation alone is never effective. This opinion is sustained by canons 11 and 15 with reference to invalidating and disqualifying laws.

[40] Coronata, I, n. 285, 2°. This is indicated constantly by Eagleton, who wrote *ex professo* on these faculties. Cf., e. g., pp. 38-39, 45-47 of his work.

[41] Canon 72—"§ 1. Privilegia cessant per renuntiationem a competente Superiore acceptatam. § 2. Privilegio in sui tantum favorem constituto quaevis persona privata renuntiare potest."

wording of canon 72, § 1, and is supported by the opinion of Van Hove.[42]

Motry (d. 1952), although he admitted that a renunciation of faculties is unusual, also concurred with this opinion. He stated that in certain instances the act of renunciation would be disrespectful to the grantor and, most probably, disadvantageous or even harmful for the many who could benefit by the application of concessions.[43] Eagleton, who wrote *ex professo* on the Quinquennial Faculties, does not express himself clearly on the opinion just alleged. He lists renunciation by the grantee among the causes extinguishing the Quinquennial Faculties. However, on the following page, he states "it is doubtful whether an ordinary could renounce faculties once they were accepted." Then further on he concludes from canon 73 that the "ordinary is not free to renounce, reject or remit those faculties which contain privileges to be used in favor of his subjects or territory."[44] Admittedly the ordinary is not free, but to say that the legal capacity of renouncing is denied seems to go beyond the purview of both canon 207, § 1 and canon 72, §§ 1, 2, 3. This same conclusion is applicable to all concessions of habitual delegation.

A similar question emerges from a consideration of particular delegation conceded to a person primarily because of the office or dignity that he possesses. This real delegation, in distinction to personal delegation, would seem, by analogy, to be subject to the ruling of canon 72, § 3. If so, then for the reasons just advanced above, this real delegation can also be renounced. To object that in this case, if an act of renunciation is possible, the rights of a third person may be injured is to overlook the fact that renunciatory intent alone is in no wise adequate to extinguish the delegated power. Or to object that the rights of the successor to the office or dignity will be prejudiced

[42] Van Hove, *De Priv.-De Disp.*, n. 244.

[43] Motry, p. 39. For this he even cited canon 72.

[44] Eagleton, pp. 45-46.

is to overlook that a concession of delegated jurisdiction is purely gratuitous. Moreover, a mere non-acceptance on the part of the grantor will furnish the needed safeguard in both contingencies.

4. The fourth consideration pertaining to the renunciation on the part of the delegate is based on the words of canon 207, § 1, namely, *deleganti directe intimata.* By this provision of the law it is necessary that the one who renounces his delegation will not only manifest his renunciatory will externally, but also that this fact be brought to the attention of the delegator. The requisites reflected in the phrase *directe intimata* as explained in the article on revocation[45] will, *mutatis mutandis,* apply also to renunciation.[46] This conclusion is evident from the identity of the expressions. It should be pointed out again that this official apprisal (here on the part of the one who renounces) is absolutely necessary, even though the superior, who perchance has learned of the renunciatory intent indirectly, as by way of rumor, is willing then and there to accept the renunciation.

Upon the consideration of what is required on the part of the one renouncing, it remains to consider renunciation *in actu secundo,* or in its effect. This calls for an analysis of the concluding phrase, *"et ab eodem* [*delegante*] *acceptata."* Three questions are revelant: 1) to whom should the act of renunciation be made, or who may accept it, 2) what constitutes the act of acceptance, and 3) what is its effect?

1. Canon 207, § 1 simply states that, if the delegated power is to become extinguished, then knowledge of the act of renunciation must be brought officially to the delegator and be accepted by him. Therefore, the first and foremost person to be apprised of the situation is the one who has granted the delegated power which the delegate

[45] Cf. *supra,* pp. 68-70.

[46] D'Annibale, I, n. 77, 3°; Vermeersch-Creusen, I, n. 322, 4°; Coronata, I, n. 290, 5°.

is attempting to renounce. Hence, if the immediate source of delegated power is the Holy See, the fact of the act of renunciation must be brought to the knowledge of the Holy See; if it is the local ordinary, to the same local ordinary.

Because of the hierarchy of jurisdiction it is correct to maintain that the renunciatory will could be made to and acceptance given by the superior of the delegator. Of course, this superior must be such in jurisdiction over the matter delegated.[47] The same prerogative is enjoyed by the successor of the one who delegated,[48] as well as by a delegate who may be designated by either of these to receive the intimation and give acceptance.

A delegate who has legitimately subdelegated part of his power is able to give effect to the renunciation on the part of the subdelegate. The same does not apply to the delegate who, when he has totally subdelegated his power and the matter has been given a legal effect by the subdelegate, is thereby considered to have abdicated his entire delegated power.[49]

2. Regarding the question about the act of acceptance, the subsequent observations are offered. The word *acceptance* generically connotes the receiving with a consenting mind what has been offered. That the word has this meaning in canon 207, § 1 is most evident.

This statement on renunciation does not specify any particular requisites for the act of acceptance. Hence it is possible for the delegated power to cease immediately upon the intimation to the delegator. It is equally possible that the act of acceptance is not elicited for several days, or a week, or even longer, and therefore the delegated power will of necessity endure for that length of time. Moreover, despite the practical difficulties that may easily arise, according to Coronata and Jone, it seems to be be-

[47] Roelker, pp. 109-110.

[48] Reg. 46, R. J., in VI°—"Is, qui in ius succedit alterius, eo iure, quo ille, uti debebit."

[49] Cf. *supra*, pp. 72-74, where it was indicated that this teaching rests on the pre-Code jurisprudence.

yond the scope of the terms used in canon 207, § 1 with reference to renunciation, to hold that the delegate must be informed of this act of acceptance by the delegator.[50] Granted that the act of renunciation and the intimation of it to the delegator have occurred, the cessation of the delegated power, according to their statements, seems to occur *ipso facto* upon the mere internal act of acceptance.

In the light of this apparent automatic effect and with a view to the obviating of practical difficulties, one could think that some kind of presumption of acceptance should arise, for otherwise the factual existence of delegated power could remain uncertain, and hence the validity of acts placed in virtue of that delegated power could remain shrouded with uncertainty.

Though this appears to be a felicitous solution, there is no legal foundation for such a presumption. It may seem that canon 200, § 2 implies this presumption. In this canon the burden of proof is put on the delegate claiming to possess delegated power.[51] Not knowing whether acceptance has or has not been given, he could not fully prove his status, and therefore the presumption could arise that he is not a delegate. This reasoning overlooks an important fact. Passing over the minor, the major premise requires a distinction. If the delegate was not able, prior to a renunciatory consideration, to prove his status, then the conclusion would be correct. But if *de facto* his claim to delegated power was provable prior to any renunciatory consideration, what is to prevent his utilizing that same proof after the renunciation on his part? Certainly his act of renunciation does not alter the proof, because *de facto* he remains a delegate at least until acceptance has been accorded his act of renunciation.[52]

In order to dispose of the difficulties that arise from the

[50] Coronata, I, n. 290, 5°; Jone, I, 207.

[51] Canon 200, § 2—"Ei, qui delegatum se asserit, incumbit onus probandae delegationis."

[52] Augustine, II, 189; Maroto, I, n. 713, II.

uncertainty about the factual existence or non-existence of the delegated power, may one not look to the following solution, which is based on the interrelation between the statements on renunciation and revocation?

In the article on revocation it was seen that the will of the delegator was all-powerful in extinguishing the gratuitous delegated power. The law, however, established an invalidating suspensive effect for the revocatory will of the delegator until that will was officially manifested to the delegate. In renunciation it is clearly the complying will of the delegator that extinguishes the delegated power. Basically, therefore, it seems that there is only an accidental or modal difference between renunciation and revocation, depending merely on the initiator of the process.

In revocation it is the will of the grantor that initiates the acts leading to the cessation of the delegated power. In renunciation it is will of the delegate that initiates the acts leading to the cessation of the delegated power. In both instances, however, it is the will of the grantor that produces the effect, namely, the cessation of the delegated power. Therefore, it seems that the statement of the law on renunciation is to be taken in conjunction with the statement of the law on revocation. And therefore a direct intimation of the acceptance of the renunciation would be required, the same invalidating suspensive effect obtaining in the case. Perhaps this is indicated in canon 207, § 1 by the proximity of the two statements. The logical sequence of the canon is clearly interrupted through the inserting of the notion of renunciation after the notion of revocation, at which point the canon reverts to a consideration of the cessation of delegated power by reason of the active subject.[53]

[53] Note the sequence. First attention is given to the cessation by reason of causes intrinsic to delegation itself (completion, time and the number of cases). Then the legislator turns to cessation by reason of the delegator or the active subject (revocation). Then consideration is given to the passive subject (renunciation), only to return again to a consideration of the active subject (*resoluto iure delegantis*).

Another argument for this opinion, and indeed more fundamental, may be advanced. From canon 53 it may be asserted that, at least with regard to a delegate constituted such in a rescript given *in forma commissoria*, official notification must be conveyed to the prospective delegate before he is validly established as a delegate.[54] Conversely, it may be argued that official knowledge is necessary before one becomes dislodged from the position of a delegate.

The necessity of the intimation of acceptance is further confirmed on analogy with the canons relating to the renunciation of an ecclesiastical office, for therein it is indicated that the act of acceptance, in order to have effect, must be intimated to the one renouncing.[55] Thus it is proposed that the word *acceptance* is best interpreted to mean not merely the acceptance as such, but to include also the notion of manifesting that intent to the one renouncing.[56]

Moreover, to maintain that no intimation of the fact of acceptance is necessary, or, in other words, to hold that the cessation of delegated power is *ipso facto* accomplished by a mere acceptance of the renunciation, seems to involve a legal inconsistency. When the provision requiring an official intimation is by law necessitated for a valid and effective revocation, this legal enactment, although not intrinsically necessary according to the fundamental notion of delegation, seems to be inserted precisely for the purpose of removing all uncertanity about the validity of acts

[54] Canon 53—"Rescripti exsecutor invalide munere suo fungitur, antequam litteras receperit earumque authenticitatem et integritatem recognoverit, nisi praevia earundem notitia ad eum fuerit auctoritate rescribentis transmissa." It is the will of the grantor that radically constitutes one as a voluntary executor, nevertheless, for the exercise of that power, knowledge of that will is now legally necessary. Cf. Van Hove, *De Rescr.*, pp. 244-245.

[55] Canons 190, 191, § 1. Blat (II, n. 156) and Crnica (I, p. 203) directly appeal to these canons for an interpretation of the statement of canon 207, § 1 on renunciation.

[56] Cf. McDevitt, pp. 106-110; Bastnagel, "Temporal Limits for Revoking Resignation from Office," *The Jurist*, IX (1949), 408-412.

placed by the delegate. This uncertainty would always be present, because perhaps altogether unbeknown to the delegate his power may have been revoked.

This uncertainty and detriment to the common good also arises relative to renunciation. The law requires the intimation of an act of renunciation and still renders the attempted renunciation invalid and ineffective until it is accepted by the delegator. Hence acts placed subsequent to the intimation of the renunciatory will of the delegate, but prior to the act of acceptance by the delegator, are most clearly valid. But unless official intimation of the acceptance is also required, the acts placed by the delegate become uncertain, since he has no way of knowing whether *de facto* the act of acceptance has occurred.

Furthermore, to say that no official intimation of the acceptance is required seems to redound to legal absurdity. If official intimation were not necessary, then it would seem that a mere internal acceptance would suffice to bring about an external juridic effect. If rumor or mere hearsay, or any other unofficial (indirect) knowledge on the part of the delegate is legally insufficient to produce an external juridic effect, namely the cessation of delegated power by reason of revocation, how much less effective in legal contemplation is a mere internal act? It alone certainly could not bring about an external juridic effect.

Against this opinion one might object that the difficulty is merely imaginative, since it is obviated by the use of jurisdiction supplied in instances of common error or positive and probable doubt.[57] Such an objection is a *petitio principii*. The benign concession of supplied jurisdiction is not to be considered as reflecting the ordinary norm. It is an exceptional device which seeks to redeem a situation created by mistake or accidental uncertainty. Why would the legislator take effective means to obviate all uncertainty and harm that may rise in the case of revocation, and then directly create occasion for the same uncertainty and harm,

[57] Canon 209.

leaving only the exceptional means of canon 209 to be used in the case of renunciation? The question is not whether canon 209 could apply to the matter of renunciation, but whether the legislator intended it to be the ordinary means for protecting the common good in this case.

It might also be objected that the alleged opinion is devoid of extrinsic authority, and is therefore improbable. As to its first part, this objection is undeniable. It is admitted that without exception every author consulted was found to state, in so many words, that acts placed after the acceptance are invalid.[58] However, these authors do not explain the meaning or content of the word *"acceptance."* Therefore, it should be noted that their statements furnish but an argument that is based on silence, since they prescind entirely from the point at issue. To cite them as opposed to this view is as improper as to cite them in affirmation of it.

Two authors were found to mention this question of intimation expressly.[59] These two, Coronata and Jone, merely state that intimation to the delegate is not required. But, as to the second part of the objection, namely that the alleged opinion is improbable in consequence of the absence of extrinsic authority, suffice to say that what is gratuitously affirmed may be gratuitiously denied. None of the authors, Coronata and Jone not excepted, advance a single reason why in this instance acceptance alone suffices, or why intimation is not necessary.

Another objection derives from the silence of canon 207, § 1 on renunciation. If intimation were legally necessary, the legislator would have expressed that fact by inserting the appropriate clause. The alleged opinion holds that this intimation is indicated not only by the proximity of the statements on renunciation and revocation and an

[58] Augustine, II, 189; Romani, I, n. 324, e; Ramstein, p. 167; Kearney, p. 115; Maroto, I, n. 713, II; Toso, Lib. II, Tom. I, p. 176; Cappello, *Summa*, I, n. 258, 5°; Ayrinhac, *General Legislation*, p. 367; Chelodi, n. 129, d.

[59] Coronata, I, n. 290, 5°; Jone, I, 207.

analysis of their application, but also on analogy with the canons on the renunciation of an ecclesiastical office. Therefore the insertion of a special clause was not necessary.

3. The third question that arises from a consideration of renunciation from the viewpoint of the delegator is this. What is the effect of the act of acceptance? First, attention will be given to the statements and conclusions of the commentators; then these observations will be applied to the opinion the writer presented above.

The necessity of acceptance on the part of the delegator is indispensable, for that appears as the expressed will of the legislator. This is shown in the words, *et ab eodem* [*delegante*] *acceptata*. Hence, even though the delegator is not able to refuse his acceptance, e.g., in the instance of a non-subject (over whom he has no jurisdictional authority), it still is necessary.[60] This example and every other case requires acceptance, because no delegate is able to free himself of the delegated power without the concurring will of the grantor.[61] This requirement follows from the nature of delegated power, which in every instance arises because of the will of the grantor.

From these remarks it is concluded that acts placed prior to acceptance are indeed valid, so that, should the acceptance be refused, then the delegated power endures.[62] Even the act of recalling one's own former renunciatory will that had been directly intimated to but not yet accepted by the delegator would be valid.[63]

Note that thus far every statement is in conformity with the opinion offered by the writer. Even the state-

[60] Maroto, I, n. 713, II; Augustine, II, 189; Coronata, I, n. 290, 5°; Ayrinhac, *General Legislation*, p. 367; Jone, I, 207.

[61] Cf. Toso, Lib. II, Tom. I, p. 176; Maroto, I, n. 713, II. Note that in the instance of a delegate empowered to subdelegate totally and in which the subdelegated matter ceases to be integral, the concurring will of the original delegator is contained in his permission to subdelegate, although this will is antecedent. This case, however, is an exception founded on pre-Code jurisprudence.

[62] Kearney, p. 115; Ramstein, p. 167; Maroto, I, n. 713, II.

[63] Chelodi, n. 129; Cappello, *Summa*, I, n. 258, 5°.

ment that acts placed after the acceptance are invalid[64] is not necessarily to be considered as opposed to the proposed opinion. The writer would insist, however, upon a distinction depending on the interpretation of the word *acceptance*. Hence, postulated the renunciatory will of the delegate and its direct intimation, exception would be taken to the statement if it implied that acts placed after a mere acceptance alone are invalid.

It should be noted that no such direct statement is advanced by the authors cited in this article. According to the opinion proposed by the writer, the same requirements would be demanded in the intimation of acceptance to the delegate as are required for the intimation of the renunciatory will of the delegate to the delegator, or of the revocatory will of the delegator to the delegate. In other words, the provision *"directe intimata"* must be verified in conjunction with the acceptance.

Upon this treatment of renunciation from the viewpoint of the delegate and the delegator, there remain several incidental questions. The necessity of a just cause for eliciting the renunciatory will is not touched by the commentators, nor is it mentioned in the law concerning the renunciation of delegated power. Nevertheless the law does not countenance capricious action in anyone, and therefore it is reasonable that some cause, proportionate to the gravity of the case, be present. In practice the delegator could and would insist that the one who renounces his delegated power advance some reason for desiring to free himself from the commission.

Relative to the question regarding matter that is no longer integral and intact, it may be stated that steps to initiate the process of renunciation may be placed at any time, regardless of the state of the delegated power. Thus, whether the delegated matter is integral and intact, or whether it has been given a legal effect, the delegated

[64] Coronata, I, n. 290, 5°.

matter is subject to the renunciatory will of the delegate.[65]

ARTICLE 2. *Resoluto Iure Delegati*

From the viewpoint of the passive subject or the delegate himself, the Code in canon 207, § 1 has listed renunciation among the causes which extinguish delegated power. From this same viewpoint, a second means may be considered, even though no mention of it is made in canon 207, § 1. This second means, by analogy to the concluding words of the same paragraph, may be entitled *Resoluto Iure Delegati*,[66] that is to say, delegated power is extinguished when the right to act is extinguished in the delegate. Obviously this demise of the right to act occurs in the instance of revocation of the delegated power, or by completion of the mandate, or, in other words, in each of the various ways previously treated. But here the reader is asked to prescind from these. The comprehension of this article, therefore, is the cessation of delegated power by reason of some act or condition of the delegated person.

Of primary concern here are the divergent conditions which may encompass the delegate and in consequence extinguish his delegated power. The first and evident condition that strikes the attention is death. What effect has death on the delegate's power? In this context the word may be used in the generic sense, so as to include not merely actual physical death, but also what analogously may be called legal or civil death.

In the first place will be considered the physical death of the delegate and its effect on his power, and secondly, the effect of the diversified legal deaths, e.g., a) the loss of a dignity or office on account of which the delegated power was given, b) the incurring of an ecclesiastical censure, c) the incurring of a vindicative penalty, and then lastly d) a summary consideration of several circum-

[65] Coronata, I, n. 290, 5°.

[66] Cf. Brys, I, n. 376, I, *in fine*, and Coronata, I, n. 290, 8°, *in fine*, who so designate it.

stances which do not necessarily extinguish delegated power, but render it inoperative in the contemplated circumstances.

Section I. Physical Death

Because Decretal legislation and subsequent jurisprudence is in harmony with the general provisions of the Code in canons 58 and 66, in virtue of canon 6 they, therefore, remain effective. This Decretal Law is found in a letter of Alexander III (1159-1181) in which he stated, in effect, that delegated jurisdiction was extinguished by the death of the delegate, unless the commission was given *intuitu dignitatis*, in which event the power passed on to the successor in the dignity.[67]

This general statement necessitates a distinction relative to the concession of delegated power, which distinction, and even the terminology, is not found wanting even among the earliest decretalists. Thus Panormitanus (1386-1453) held that delegated power was to be designated as real when it contemplated the person's dignity or office, and personal when it looked to a specified individual as its possessor or bearer.[68] Or again, according to Gonzalez-Tellez (fl. 1673), a real delegation looked to the dignity or office of the person delegated, while a personal delegation attended to the personal qualifications (i.e., *industria personae*) of the intended bearer.[69]

Whether delegation is real or personal will depend upon the letter of delegation which should clearly manifest the intention of the grantor through the use of a specific word-

[67] C. 14, X, *de officio et potestate iudicis delegati,* I, 29; Jaffé, n. 14175. Cf. Gonzalez-Tellez, lib. I, tit. XXIX, c. XIV, n. 9.

[68] Panormitanus, lib. I, tit. XXIX, c. XIV, n. 4. Cf. also Sandaeus, lib. I, tit. XXIX, c. XIV, n. 1; *Glossa Ordinaria* ad c. 14, *eo. loc.*, s. v. *substitutum.*

[69] Gonzalez-Tellez, lib. I, tit. XXIX, c. XIV, n. 8. A comparison of this definition of personal delegation with that of Panormitanus' indicates a distinction respectively between merely personal and strictly personal delegation, which distinction, in relation to the cessation of delegated power, is unimportant.

ing. If the words therein used fail in this regard, then the circumstances surrounding the concession of the delegated power are to be examined for the ascertainment of this will.[70] This same procedure is given legal force today in virtue of canon 18. If, however, the solution remains doubtful, then there arises a presumption that the delegation is personal.[71] This presumption is based on the pre-Code jurisprudence which held that all delegated power, since it derogated from ordinary jurisdiction, was to be deemed of an odious character, and therefore was to receive a restrictive interpretation.[72] According to the Code this is confirmed by canon 200, § 1, in the instance of a particular delegation, which receives a strict interpretation.[73]

[70] Sebastianelli, *De Personis,* pars 1, n. 126.

[71] Sebastianelli, *loc. cit.;* Panormitanus, lib. I, tit. XXIX, c. XIV, n. 4; Sanchez, lib. VIII, disp. XXVII, n. 17; Pirhing, lib. I, tit. XXIX, n. 167; Reiffenstuel, lib. I, tit. XXIX, n. 128. The doubtful situation of which these authors treated was that in which delegation was given both with the expressed name of the person's dignity and with the expressed name of the person then possessing the dignity. Sanchez (*loc. cit.*) listed four opinions on this question, summarily dismissing the first three. The first opinion held that the commission was presumptively real, because the quality of the dignity prevails over the quality of the person. The second held that with whatever expression preceded the commission was in accord. The third opinion was based on the knowledge of the grantor. If he knew the delegated person, then the grant was a personal one, and if he did not know him, *in re dubia* the grant was always to be understood as accorded to the dignity. The fourth opinion held that generally the genus was determined and restricted by what preceded or followed it. Hence, when the more generic signification of the dignity was used in conjunction with the specific name of the person, the determination was implemented through the latter. Moreover, all words in the letter of delegation were to have a bearing on the subject; superfluous words were not to be inserted. Thus a delegation, if both the generic name of a dignity or office and the specific name of the person were used, was in doubtful cases rendered intelligible only if it was considered personal in character.

[72] Reiffenstuel, lib. I, tit. XXIX, n. 52; Sanchez, lib. III, disp. XXXV, n. 9.

[73] Canon 200, § 1—"Potestas iurisdictionis ordinaria et ad uni-

If one bear in mind the distinction between real delegation and personal delegation, be it strictly or merely personal, their cessation is as follows. The death of the delegate extinguishes all the delegated jurisdiction insofar as the delegate is concerned. This is most evident from the very law of nature. If one consider delegated power as such, strictly personal delegated power (*ea quae commissa est personae, industriae personae*)[74] ceases by the death of the delegate, since it cannot be perpetuated by being transferred or subdelegated to another at the hand of the delegate.[75] Even merely personal delegation (*ea quae commissa est personae, non industriae personae, necnon intuitu dignitatis vel officii*)[76] ceases by the death of the delegate, since it adheres to the person and suffers the same fate as the person. If a merely personal delegation has been legitimately subdelegated to another, its cessation on the part of the subdelegate will be governed by the norms given in the article *Resoluto Iure Delegantis.* The termination of all personal delegation follows the Rule of Law, *Accessorium naturam sequi congruit principalis.*[77]

These conclusions are directly inferred from the Decretal Law[78] and, moreover, may also be negatively deduced from canon 58, which permits the execution of a rescript

versitatem negotiorum delegata, late interpretanda est; alia quaelibet stricte; . . . ." Maroto (I, n. 714, II) advanced what appears to be an unwarranted distinction. He stated: "1°. In dubio, cum res sint ad bonum animarum directae et favorabiles praesumuntur, nisi contrarium certo constet, *reales* ac proinde transeunt ad successores, si vero sint odiosae et contineant restrictionem iurisdictionis ordinariae praesumuntur *personales.*"

[74] Cf. *supra* pp. 18-19.

[75] Canon 199, § 2. Cf. also canon 58. Brys (I, n. 367, I, *in fine*) and Bouuaert-Simenon (I, n. 361, I, *in fine*) state that only strictly personal delegation ceases by the death of the delegate, but the context indicates that the word "*stricte*" is used only in apposition to real.

[76] Cf. *supra,* pp. 18-19.

[77] Reg. 42, R. J., in VI°. Cf. Panormitanus, lib. I, tit. XXIX, c. XIV, n. 4; Ferraris, s. v. *delegare,* n. 42.

[78] C. 24, X, *de officio et potestate iudicis delegati,* I, 29. This decretal specifically spoke of the perpetuity of a real delegation.

to be accomplished by the successor in the office or dignity previously possessed by the executor, unless the executor had been selected because of personal qualifications.[79] These conclusions are the common teaching of the post-Code authors,[80] in line with what was constantly taught before the Code.[81]

Real delegation is not extinguished by the death of the delegate possessing it. It is conceded to the person because of the office or dignity which he possesses, and hence it is said to adhere to the dignity or the office rather than to the person.[82] For this reason real delegation is perpetuated for the successor in the office or dignity, since obviously the office or dignity does not cease with the demise of the holder. This conclusion is manifestly evident from the legislation of Alexander III (1159-1181) and the subsequent jurisprudence of the pre-Code authors,[83] as well as the canonical writers since the Code.[84]

Section II. Juridical Death

Besides physical death there occurs what may be called civil or legal death, in the sense that with respect to the office or dignity, or the faculty of acting jurisdictionally, the former possessor is by the law regarded as of a status

[79] Canon 58—"Rescripta quaelibet exsecutioni mandari possunt etiam ab exsecutoris successore in dignitate vel officio, nisi fuerit electa industria personae."

[80] Kearney, p. 115; Lega-Bartoccetti, I, p. 203; Maroto, I, n. 714, II; Brys, I, n. 367, I, *in fine;* Bouuaert-Simenon, I, n. 361, I, *in fine;* Prümmer, p. 123; Cocchi, Lib. II, Pars I, p. 246; Romani, I, n. 324, h; Beste, p. 221; *et alii.*

[81] No author was found to deny this. To cite but a few, e.g., Boich, *In Quinque Decretalium Libros Commentaria* (Venetiis, 1576), super 1° decret. *de officio et potestate iudicis delgati,* s. v. *quoniam abbas,* n. 10 (hereafter cited Boich); Barbosa, lib. I, tit. XXIX, c. XIV, nn. 4-6; Veranus, *Juris Canonici Universi Commentarius Paratitlaris* (5 vols., Monachii, 1703-1708), lib. I, tit. XXIX, § VI, n. 11 (hereafter cited Veranus); Santi-Leitner, lib. I, tit. XXIX, n. 33; Bouix, pars 1, p. 159.

[82] Maroto, I, n. 714, II.

[83] For authors cf. *supra,* in footnote 81.

[84] For authors cf. *supra,* in footnote 80.

equivalent to that of the dead. Successively there will be considered: a) the loss of the dignity or the office to which the delegated power was attached, b) the effect of ecclesiastical censures, c) the effect of the vindicative penalty of deposition, and then briefly d) the factors deriving from conditional mandates, incompetence, and from the exception of suspicion.

A. The Loss of Dignity or Office

In the instance of real delegation, it is clearly evident that the power of the delegate ceases when he loses the office or dignity on account of which the delegated power was conferred upon him. This follows as a corollary to what has just been stated above. The delegated power is looked upon as adhering to the office or dignity and as participated in by the person only because he possesses the office or dignity. Consequently if the delegate is removed or deposed or for any reason loses the office or dignity, *eo ipso* there perishes the power he enjoyed as deriving from that dignity or office.[85]

B. The Effect of Ecclesiastical Censures

What effect the delegate's lapse into an ecclesiastical censure would have on his delegated power is not indicated in canon 207, § 1, nor do the commentators of the Code generally advert to this possibility in their commentary on delegated jurisdiction.[86] Indirectly this possibility is mentioned when consideration is given to the requisites for delegation on the part of the passive subject. It was there stated that, among other qualifications, the prospective delegate must not be under any ecclesiastical penalty, which renders the acquisition of delegated power sometimes invalid and sometimes illicit. So also the retention of delegated power is affected by ecclesiastical censures.

[85] Ferraris, s. v. *delegare*, nn. 54-55; Maroto, I, n. 714, II.

[86] Coronata was found to mention this effect, but, as will be seen, his statement is too extensive.—Cf. I, n. 290, 8°.

Excommunication: Concerning the effect of excommunication on jurisdiction, Hyland, who wrote *ex professo* on the subject, presents the following in summary of the pre-Code teaching.[87]

> "All excommunicates were deprived of ecclesiastical jurisdiction in such a manner that they could not exercise acts thereof, at least licitly. The reason was because the exercise of jurisdiction is *praecipua cum fidelibus communicatio*.... All authors agreed that the *vitandi* were altogether stripped of ecclesiastical jurisdiction. Consequently, acts of jurisdiction placed by them were invalid. Jurisdiction for the internal forum was restored to them for the extreme necessity of the moment of death. The *tolerati* were not altogether stripped of the power of jurisdiction, but they were forbidden to exercise acts thereof. Even if they were publicly known to be under the ban of excommunication, they could validly exercise jurisdiction, as long as they were not objected to by the faithful.... Acts of jurisdiction posited by the *tolerati* at the request of the faithful were not only valid, but licit as well."[88]

According to the Code an excommunication excludes one from communion with the other members of the Church,[89] and accordingly it seems that the deprivation of jurisdiction ought also to be effected. However, for the common good of the same society, the legislator has provided that

[87] Hyland, *Excommunication, Its Nature, Historical Development and Effects*, The Catholic University of America Canon Law Studies, n. 49 (Washington, D. C.: The Catholic University of America, 1928), pp. 145-146 (hereafter cited Hyland).

[88] These conclusions are sustained by the following authors: Boich, super I° decret. *de sententia et re iudicata*, s. v. *ad probandum*, nn. 1-5; Hostiensis, lib. V, *de sent. excommunicationis*, n. 1; Pichler, lib. V, tit. XXXIX, n. 29; Engel, *Collegium Universi Juris Canonici* (7. ed., Venetiis, 1733), lib. V, tit. XXXIX, n. 55 (hereafter cited Engel); Veranus, lib. I, tit. XXIX, § VI, n. 6; Grandclaude, *Jus Canonicum juxta Ordinem Decretalium* (3 vols., Parisiis, 1882-1883), lib. V, tit. XXXIX, p. 594 (hereafter cited Grandclaude); Santi-Leitner, lib. V, tit. XXXIX, n. 34, V; *et alii.*

[89] Canon 2257, § 1.

only the *vitandi* are completely deprived of jurisdiction, so that their acts, subsequent to the sentence, are invalid.[90]

The *tolerati* who are excommunicated upon a condemnatory or a declaratory sentence seem to be *inhabiles* for receiving delegated jurisdiction.[90a] However, the delegated power obtained prior to the infliction of the censure does not cease when the censure is inflicted, as is deducible from canon 2266. The exercise of that delegated power is rendered invalid by canon 2264.[91] Hence, unlike the *vitandus,* the *toleratus* does not lose his delegated power; its exercise is merely suspended together with an invalidating effect, so that when the censure is removed, no new grant of delegated power is required in order that he may effectively place jurisdictional acts. The delegated power of the simple *toleratus* (i.e., when no sentence has intervened) is likewise suspended, but only with an effect that touches the licitness of the acts, as is indicated in canon 2264.

Moreover, by the benign exceptional provision the faithful in danger of death (*in solo mortis periculo*) are able to ask not only the *tolerati* under sentence but even the *vitandi* for sacramental absolution. In this instance their exercise of jurisdiction is valid as well as licit according to canon 2261, § 3. According to paragraph 2 of the same

[90] Canon 2266—"Post sententiam condemnatoriam vel declaratoriam excommunicatus manet privatus fructibus dignitatis, officii, beneficii, pensionis, muneris, si quod habeat in Ecclesia; et vitandus ipsamet dignitate, officio, beneficio, pensione, munere." Roberti correctly points out that the *ipso facto vitandus* of canon 2343, § 1, 1°, for his laying of violent hands on the Holy Father, would not be automatically deprived of his delegated jurisdiction; this deprivation would have to come as the effect of a declaratory or a condemnatory sentence. Cf. Roberti, *De Delictis et Poenis* (Vol. 1, Pars II, ed. altera, Romae: Apud Custodiam Librariam Pontificii Instituti Utriusque Iuris, 1944), n. 328 (hereafter cited *De Delictis et Poenis*).

[90a] Cf. canon 2265, § 1, 2°.

[91] Canon 2264—"Actus iurisdictionis tam fori externi quam fori interni positus ab excommunicato est illicitus; et, si lata fuerit sententia condemnatoria vel declaratoria, etiam invalidus, salvo praescripto can. 2261, § 3; secus est validus, imo etiam licitus, si a fidelibus petitus sit ad normam mem. can. 2261, § 2."

canon the sacramental absolution of the simple *toleratus* is rendered licit whenever the faithful, for any just reason, request his ministration, especially if no other minister is available.[92]

Suspension: Prior to the Code the effect of this censure on jurisdiction depended on the type of suspension that was incurred, but at most the effect was merely one of a prohibitory character.[93] The present law has not changed this effect. Rainer, who wrote expressly on the subject of suspension, indicates that the suspended cleric may not administer the sacraments or exercise any jurisdiction, unless the law permits such an exercise or administration for certain designated cases. In order to have a prohibitory effect on jurisdiction, the suspension must be a general suspension, a suspension *ab officio,* or a suspension *a iurisdictione.*[94]

Moreover, when one has incurred a censure which forbids the administration of the sacraments, the exceptions of canon 2261 are applicable. If there has been incurred a suspension which forbids the placing of an act of jurisdiction, whether in the internal or in the external forum, the act is nevertheless valid, unless a condemnatory or a declaratory sentence has intervened, or unless the superior express-

92 More detailed treatment of the effect of excommunication according to the Code may be found in Roberti, *De Delictis et Poenis,* n. 328; Ayrinhac-Lydon, *Penal Legislation in the New Code of Canon Law* (revised ed., New York, Boston, Cincinnati, Chicago, San Francisco: Denziger Brothers, Inc., 1944), nn. 120-122; Maroto, I, n. 576, D-E; Hyland, pp. 146-149; Vermeersch-Creusen, III, nn. 468-469; Coronata, IV, nn. 1779-1781. Cappello (*De Sacramentis,* V, n. 662) indicates that the same effect is had on the power of assisting at marriages.

93 Cf. Engel, lib. V, tit. XXXIX, nn. 73-78; Reiffenstuel, lib. V, tit. XXXIX, n. 159; Wernz, VI, n. 208; Liguori, *Theologia Moralis* (2 vols., Augustae Taurinorum, 1891), II, nn. 312-314, 333 (hereafter cited Liguori).

94 Canons 2278, § 2; 2279, § 1, § 2, 1°. Cf. also Rainer, *Suspension of Clerics,* The Catholic University of America Canon Law Studies, n. 111 (Washington, D. C.: The Catholic University of America, 1937), pp. 37, 78-79 (hereafter cited Rainer); Woywod, II, 452-453.

ly declared that he revoked the jurisdiction itself. If no condemnatory or declaratory sentence has intervened, the acts are illicit, unless they are performed at the request of the faithful according to the norms of canon 2261, § 2.[95]

Interdict: The pre-Code jurisprudence concerning the effect of interdict on jurisdiction paralleled that which regarded the effect of suspension: in both instances the effect was of a merely prohibitory character,[96] at least with regard to the needed jurisdiction for the sacrament of penance, since generally an interdict brought with it a prohibition against the administration of the sacraments.[97]

The Code has prohibited the administration of the sacraments by one who is personally interdicted. Hence, when jurisdiction is required in this administration, the exercise of that jurisdiction is forbidden, except of course for the provisions of canon 2261.[98] Moreover, when this penalty has been inflicted with a declaratory or a condemnatory sentence, any exercise of jurisdiction, except within the compass of canon 2261, §§ 2, 3, is attended with invalidity.[98a]

C. The Effect of Vindicative Penalties

Under this heading need be considered only deposition, since generally it is the first among the vindicative penal-

[95] Canon 2284—"Si incursa fuerit censura suspensionis quae vetat administrationem Sacramentorum et Sacramentalium, servetur praescriptum can. 2261; si censura suspensionis quae prohibet actum iurisdictionis in foro seu interno seu externo, actus est invalidus, ex. gr., absolutio sacramentalis, si lata sit sententia condemnatoria vel declaratoria, aut Superior expresse declaret se ipsam iurisdictionis potestatem revocare; secus est illicitus tantum, nisi a fidelibus petitus fuerit ad normam mem. can. 2261, § 2." For a comprehensive treatment of the effect of suspension, cf. Rainer, pp. 58-112.

[96] Pichler, lib. V, tit. XXXIX, n. 50; Suarez, Vol. 22, disp. XV, sect. IV, n. 6; disp. XXXIII, proem. ad sect. I.

[97] Roberti, *De delictis et Poenis*, n. 347, II.

[98] Canon 2275—"Personaliter interdicti: ... 2.° Prohibentur Sacramenta et Sacramentalia ministrare, conficere et recipere, ad normam can. 2260, § 1, 2261." Cf. Roberti, *op. cit.*, n. 352, B-C.

[98a] Canon 2275, 3°.

ties that affect jurisdiction. Moreover, what is said of this penalty is *a fortiori* applicable not only to the more severe vindicative penalty of perpetual deprivation of the clerical garb, but also that of degradation.

The jurisprudence of the earlier law on the question of the relationship between delegated jurisdiction and the vindicative penalty of deposition is summarized by Findlay.[99]

> "Thus it is evident that deposition deprived the cleric of the lawful use of his powers of orders. It also deprived him of his office and jurisdiction. The powers of jurisdiction, however, he lost completely, for these, unlike the powers of orders, depended exclusively on the will of the legislative authority in the Church. All the acts of jurisdiction which he ventured to accomplish after deposition were null and void. While suspension deprived a cleric of his use of jurisdiction, deposition went further and deprived him of the jurisdiction itself, as well as of the office he enjoyed in the Church."[100]

The Code has left this provision unchanged. The deposition of a cleric deprives him permanently of all offices, benefices, dignities, pensions and functions in the Church, and moreover it deprives him of the subjective capacity to acquire them in the future.[101] Therefore, every delegated jurisdiction ceases entirely in the cleric who is deposed,

[99] Findlay, *Canonical Norms Governing the Deposition and Degradation of Clerics*, The Catholic University of America Canon Law Studies, n. 130 (Washington, D. C.: The Catholic University of America Press, 1941), p. 74 (hereafter cited Findlay).

[100] This expressly refers to the teaching prior to the Council of Trent, but this effect remained unchanged during the period from the Council of Trent to the Code, as Findlay states on p. 93. Cf. also Durandus, lib. I, partic. I, *de iudice delegato*, § 6, n. 7; Panormitanus, lib. I, tit. XXIX, c. XXX, n. 7; Veranus, lib. I, tit. XXIX, § VI, n. 6; Liguori, II, nn. 323-324; Wernz, VI, nn. 125, 138.

[101] Canon 2303, § 1—"Depositio, firmis obligationibus e suscepto ordine exortis et privilegiis clericalibus, secumfert tum suspensionem ab officio, et inhabilitatem ad quaelibet officia, dignitates, beneficia, pensiones, munera in Ecclesia...."

since this penalty not only dismisses him from every office in the strict sense, but also from any other office or function.[102] The only exception to this obtains for the administration of the sacrament of penance to a person *in periculo mortis.*[103]

D. Other Factors Affecting Delegated Power

1°. Conditional Mandates. Delegated power may in its content or extension be circumscribed by the will of the grantor, and whatever conditions are manifested in the rescript of delegation, they must be observed even under pain of invalidity if the conditions are set as essential.[104] Such conditions may relate to territory, to persons, to things, etc. Generally, however, acts placed beyond the scope of the power conferred would have no effect on the stability or the instability of the power itself.

Nevertheless, it is possible for the grantor not only to append essential conditions to the rescript of delegation, but even to effect an automatic cessation of the power itself in the event that the condition is overstepped. This automatic cessation could be accomplished by means of an express clause to that effect. Such a clause would be looked upon as an antecedent revocatory will already intimated. One must read the rescript to determine the kind of power, its scope and its continued existence. If no such clause is clearly evident, as may happen in the overwhelming majority of cases, the delegate's power is merely inoperative when it transcends the jurisdictional content of the mandate.

2°. Incompetence of a Delegated Judge. Incompetence is a deficiency in the jurisdiction of a judge in relation to the cause or controversy brought to his court. This incompetence is called absolute if a judge is entirely devoid of jurisdiction over a particular case, whereas it is called relative if the judge indeed possesses jurisdiction, but *de*

[102] Findlay, p. 150.

[103] Canon 882.

[104] Canons 39; 203.

facto there is no legitimate legal title in virtue of which the judge may actually undertake or continue to hear the cause.[105] It seems needless to stress the fact that the possession of delegated power is subject to vitiation through incompetence on the part of its bearer.

The law states that a cause becomes reserved to the Roman Pontiff by the very fact that he summons it to his own tribunal.[106] Moreover, any member of the faithful may, at any stage of the trial, even in the second instance, present his cause to the Holy See, which may then reserve the cause to itself.[107] Such an action on the part of the Supreme Pontiff brings about absolute incompetence in every judge except the one chosen by the Holy See to take cognizance of the cause.[108] Hence in the instance that a cause, if legitimately committed to a delegated judge, is subsequently summoned to the Holy See, the absolute incompetence of the delegated judge would effect the cessation of his delegated power. This may be argued from the factual situation therein that the final cause for which the delegation was made can no longer be attained through this delegate by means of his former delegation.

3°. Exception of Suspicion. The exception of suspicion, or the *recusatio,* as it was called, was defined as the canonically alleged non-acceptability of a judge for the hearing of a given cause, and it was invoked because there attached to the judge the suspicion of a prejudice against a party.[109] This exception received prominent treatment at the hands of the pre-Code commentators as among the causes extinguishing delegated power. It was quite com-

105 Coyle, p. 92; Roberti, I, n. 60; Lega-Bartoccetti, I, p. 39.

106 Canon 1557, § 3.

107 Canon 1569, § 1.

108 Canons 1557, § 3; 1558.

109 Passerinus, lib. I, *de officio et potestate iudicis delegati,* c. IV, n. 2; Reiffenstuel, lib. I, tit. XXIX, n. 148; De Angelis, *Praelectiones Juris Canonici ad Methodum Decretalium Gregorii IX Exactae* (5 vols. in 9, Romae et Parisiis, 1877-1891), lib. I, tit. XXIX, n. 8, VI (hereafter cited De Angelis).

monly taught that, when this exception had been legitimately proposed and a sentence favorable to the litigant had been pronounced, then the delegate's power entirely ceased.[110]

The effect of this exception of suspicion is not clearly enunciated in the present law.[111] It is evident in the law that if the exception is sustained, the delegated judge as well as an ordinary judge is to be relieved of his duties with respect to the particular suit at court.[112] If this removal occurs, the judge delegated *ad universitatem causarum* loses his power relative to the particular cause, just as a judge delegated for a particular cause entirely loses his power when it is revoked by the delegator. However, if *de facto* the delegated judge is not relieved of his judicial duties, the question arises whether or not his subsequent judicial acts are valid.

Noone maintains that the present legislation contains no sanction of nullity against a procedure conducted by a judge declared to be suspect, and that therefore his acts cannot be said to be invalid.[113] This statement affords a very weak basis for departing from the pre-Code teaching that the decision concerning suspicion when rendered in favor of the litigant extinguished the power of the judge delegated for the cause. It does not seem improbable that

[110] Reiffenstuel, lib. I, tit. XXIX, n. 151; Wernz, II, n. 561, VII; Ferraris, s. v. *delegare*, n. 62, 8°; Bouix, pars 1, p. 162; *et alii*.

[111] Canons 1613-1617. For a brief summary of the historical background for the exception of suspicion cf. Roberti, I, n. 151.

[112] Canon 1615, § 1. Cf. also Coyle, p. 102; Roberti, I, n. 158; Coronata, III, n. 1146, 6°.

[113] Noone, p. 33-34. This statement is greatly weakened by what seems to be an inconsistency. Noone correctly holds with Roberti (I, n. 158) and Lega-Bartoccetti (I, p. 229) that the acts placed by the suspected judge while the decision concerning the suspicion is pending are *ipso facto* null, because they constitute a prejudiced attempt against the party. He does not explain, beyond the silence of the law in canon 1615, § 1, 2°, why the acts of the suspected judge appear to be valid when placed after the decision that is adverse to him. In holding the former view, he could logically have been expected to argue for the invalidity of the acts placed after the decision.

this pre-Code jurisprudence could certainly be held to-day, at least to the effect that resumption of the cause by the judge against the objection of the party would constitute an *attentatum,* and hence would be an invalid act under canons 1615, § 1; 1854 and 1855, § 1.

Furthermore, this conclusion may be indirectly deduced from the more probable opinion of Roberti and Lega-Bartoccetti who state that acts placed by a suspected judge while the decision concerning the proposed suspicion is pending are *ipso iure* null.[114] This nullity arises because of the prejudicial attempt against the party who raised the exception.[115] Upon the basis of this opinion, it may be said, *a fortiori,* that the delegated judge against whom the sentence concerning suspicion has been passed cannot place valid acts, and therefore cannot bring the cause to a valid conclusion.

This inference is conclusive if it can be maintained that the legitimate sentence of suspicion when passed in favor of the party who proposed it cannot subsequently be rescinded by this party. In other words, can this party choose to ignore the legitimate sentence of suspicion and accept the ministration of the suspect judge? If he can render this sentence legally ineffective, then it is possible that the suspect judge can proceed to place valid acts and bring the cause to a valid conclusion. This problem, being quite incidental to the present work, will not be pursued further. Suffice to say that if the party (or even the promoter of justice) confronts the judge with the sentence that confirms the exception of suspicion against the judge, the acts placed by the suspect judge will constitute a prejudicial attempt. Therefore a valid conclusion of the suit appears unattainable by the suspect judge. The purpose of the delegation being impossible of fulfillment by this judge, the delegated power relative to the cause is extinguished.

[114] Roberti, I, n. 158; Lega-Bartoccetti, I, p. 229. This opinion is denied by Wernz-Vidal (VI, n. 151) and Muñiz (II, n. 152), who hold on the basis of canon 11 that the acts are valid but rescissible.

[115] Canons 1854; 1855, § 1.

CHAPTER VI

CESSATION OF MULTIPLE DELEGATION

In canon 207, § 3 a special provision is made. It governs the cessation of power that has been delegated to a group as a unit. It states that when several persons are delegated collegiately, all lose their delegated power if one cannot act, unless a clause to the contrary is stated in the letter of delegation.[1] This paragraph indicates that the passive subject of delegated power can be, not just a single person, but even several persons. Furthermore the fact of multiple delegation or delegation given to a group is indicated in other canons of the Code.[2] Note that the statements made above concerning the requirements in the passive subject of delegation are applicable to these delegates.[3]

ARTICLE 1. HISTORICAL NOTE

Delegation made to a group for the same case was not unknown during the period of Decretal Law. Gregory IX (1227-1241) gave a clear rule in this regard. He stated that when delegation was given to several, the entire delegated power expired at the death of one of them, unless there was an express statement to the contrary.[4] The usual express clauses to the contrary were, "*quod si non omnes his exsequendis poteritis interesse,*"[5] or "*quod si omnes interesse nequiverint,*"[6] or "*quod si ambo interesse*

[1] Canon 207, § 3—"Pluribus collegialiter delegatis, si unus deficiat, aliorum quoque delegatio exspirat, nisi aliud ex tenore delegationis constet."

[2] Cf. canons 205, 206, 1576, 1577, 1614, § 1.

[3] Cf. *supra*, pp. 90-92.

[4] C. 42, X, *de officio et potestate iudicis delegati*, I, 29; Potthast, n. 9557.

[5] C. 30, X, *eo. tit.*, I, 29; Potthast, n. 3664.

[6] C. 21, § 1, X, *eo. tit.*, I, 29; Jaffé, n. 17019.

non possunt."[7] When these clauses were inserted, the absolute collegiate activity of the group in its entirety was mitigated so that, with the loss of power on the part of one, the remaining delegates could act or continue to act.[8] Multiple delegation could also be given in such a way that, while indeed several persons were deputed, still each individual was constituted with full competence to act (*in solidum*).[9]

ARTICLE 2. CANONICAL COMMENTARY

Bearing in mind the historical antecedents of multiple delegation in one's analysis of the present law, one notes that the Code has concisely and lucidly restated the former legislation. In order to properly understand the import of the law concerning multiple delegation, it is first necessary to clarify the terminology.

Multiple delegation has reference to a plurality of passive subjects receiving delegated power. It also implies that these delegates are commissioned relative to the same matter. Certainly several delegates could be named at the same time or at different times, but if they are to undertake different matters, e.g., one is delegated to dispense from a matrimonial impediment, another to judge a contentious cause, another to absolve from a censure, then a grant of multiple delegation is not made, at least not in the sense here employed. This is demonstrated by the use in canon 205 of such phrases as "*omnes simul . . . procedere debent,*" and "*qui antea negotium occupavit, alios ab eodem excludit.*" Therefore multiple delegation necessarily includes two notions, namely, a plurality of passive subjects,

[7] C. 4, *eo. tit.*, I, 14, in VI°.

[8] *Glossa Ordinaria* ad c. 21, § 1, X, *eo. tit.*, I, 29, s. v. *casus;* Panormitanus, lib. I, tit. XXIX, c. XXI, n. 1; Wernz, II, n. 557; Bouix, pars 1, n. 150; De Angelis, lib. I, tit. XXIX, n. 7.

[9] C. 8, *eo. tit.*, I, 14, in VI°; *Nuperrimae*, Vol. 6, decis. CCCLXXXV (2 julii 1700), n. 24. Cf. also Panormitanus, lib. I, tit. XXIX, c. XXI, n. 7; *Glossa Ordinaria* ad c. 8, *eo. tit.*, I, 14, in VI°, s. v. *cum plures;* Schmalzgrueber, lib. I, tit., XXIX, n. 17; Reiffenstuel, lib. I, tit. XXIX, n. 114; Wernz, II, n. 557.

all of whom are delegated in some manner for the same thing.

This plural delegation may be made simultaneously or successively, which terms are self-explanatory. Successive multiple delegation is the burden of canon 206, which states that when delegation is granted successively to several persons, he whose mandate is first in point of time ought to transact the commission, unless his mandate was expressly abrogated by the subsequent delegation of another person.[10] This is a restatement of Decretal Law[11] and is an application of the Rule of Law, *Qui prior est tempore, potior est iure.*[12]

Regatillo correctly points out that this canon does not impose an obligation of proceeding first, but merely establishes the prior delegate with a *ius praeferens* in those instances in which no abrogatory clause is used.[13] It could be disputed whether acts of the second delegate placed in violation of this *ius praeferens* are valid. In this he rightly maintains the validity of such acts, for the reason that no invalidating clause is expressed, as there is relative to collegiate delegation.[14] Hence this *ius praeferens* is not absolute. Nor is it necessarily perpetual.

Maroto (1875-1937), applying canon 48, § 2,[15] held that a second rescript, even though no abrogatory clause is expressed in it, would suspend the prior delegation if the prior delegation had not been used because of deceit or

[10] Canon 206—"Pluribus successive delegatis, ille negotium expedire debet cuius mandatum anterius est nec posteriore rescripto expresse abrogatum fuit."

[11] Cf. c. 29, X, *de officio et potestate iudicis delegati,* I, 29; Potthast, n. 325; c. 28, § 2, X, *eo. tit.*, I, 29; Potthast, n. 2350; cc. 6, 7, *eo. tit.*, I, 14, in VI°; c. 24, X, *de rescriptis,* I, 3; Potthast, n. 4072.

[12] Reg. 54, R. J., in VI°.

[13] Regatillo, I, n. 366.

[14] Regatillo, *loc. cit.*

[15] Canon 48, § 2—"Si [rescripta] sint aeque peculiaria aut generalia, prius tempore praevalet posteriori, nisi in altero fiat expressa mentio de priore, aut nisi prior impetrator dolo vel notabili negligentia suo rescripto usus non fuerit."

notable negligence.[16] Kearney uses paragraph 3 of the same canon to solve the dispute that arises when the priority in time cannot be determined.[17] It states that if the rescripts were given on the same day and it is not known which was issued first, then both are invalid and, if the matter warrants, recourse must be made to the grantor.[18] Over and above these provisions, successive multiple delegated power ceases according to the norms of canon 207, § 1.

Simultaneous multiple delegation may be granted in a two-fold manner, namely, in a collegiate manner and in a distributive manner (*in solidum facta*). The latter is that delegation which commissions several persons to undertake the same matter in such a way that each delegate is equally competent to execute the mandate by himself. It is designated as a delegation made *in solidum,* because the power is entire and firm (*solida*) in each delegate, independently of the others.[19]

The actual exercise of this kind of delegation is governed by the rule of jurisdictional priority (*locus praeventioni*), so that he who first undertakes the use of the power delegated excludes the others from the right to act in the matter, unless he is afterwards impeded or is unwilling to continue to execute the affair.[20] It should be noted that the power of the other delegates is not extinguished, but merely suspended, when one delegate begins to execute the

[16] Maroto, I, n. 708, IV; n. 286, B, b.

[17] Kearney, p. 110.

[18] Canon 48, § 3—"Quod si eodem die fuerint concessa nec liqueat uter prior impetraverit, utrumque irritum est, et, si res ferat, rursus ad eum qui rescripta dedit, est recurrendum."

[19] Maroto, I, n. 708, V, a; Cocchi, Lib. II, Pars I, p. 243.

[20] Canon 205, § 2—"Pluribus in solidum delegatis, qui antea negotium occupavit, alios ab eodem excludit, nisi aut posthac impediatur aut nolit ulterius in negotio procedere." Cf. also *Nuperrimae,* Vol. 6, decis. CCCLXXXV (2 iulii 1700), n. 24; Schmalzgrueber, lib. I, tit. XXIX, n. 17; Sebastianelli, *De Personis,* pars 1, n. 119; Ojetti, s. v. *delegatio,* n. 1736; Maroto, I, n. 708, V, a; Wernz-Vidal, II, n. 373.

matter. Should he for any reason become impeded or should he desist from acting, and this fact is authentically established by messenger, letter or witnesses,[21] then the rule of exclusive jurisdictional priority obtains again with the same suspensive effect for the power of the remaining delegates. But besides this suspensive effect, the power of one or all may actually be extinguished according to the ordinary rules of canon 207, § 1.

In addition to a distributive delegation, a collegiate delegation can reflect the fact that a simultaneous multiple delegation has been granted. A collegiate delegation implies that jurisdiction has been conferred upon several, not as individuals or independently of one another, but as a group, a unit or a college.[22] Like the Decretal Law, canon 205, § 3 provides that, for the validity of their acts, those who are commissioned collegiately are bound to proceed together in handling the delegated matter, unless other provision is made in the mandate.[23] From this paragraph it is clear that a multiple delegation may be given in an absolute or unqualified (*simpliciter*) manner and in a relative or qualified (*secundum quid*) collegiate manner.[24] The first is the one that is given without any alternate provision; the second is the result of the alternate provision as found both in canon 205, § 3 (*nisi in mandato aliud cautum sit*) and canon 207, § 3 (*nisi aliud ex tenore delegationis constet*).

This latter canon contains the norm governing the cessation of collegiate delegation. It states that when several are delegated collegiately, if the power of one becomes extinct, the delegation of the others also expires, unless the con-

[21] Kearney, p. 109; Legà-Bartoccetti, I, pp. 201-202.

[22] Panormitanus, lib. I, tit. XXIX, c. XXI, n. 7; Wernz, II, n. 557; Maroto, I, n. 708, V, b; Cocchi, Lib. II, Pars I, p. 243.

[23] Canon 205, § 3—"Pluribus collegialiter delegatis, omnes simul pro actorum validitate in negotio expediendo procedere debent, nisi in mandato aliud cautum sit."

[24] Cf. Lega-Bartoccetti, I, p. 201.

trary is evident from the very tenor of the delegation.[25] Therefore, if the collegiate delegation has been granted absolutely or without any alternate provision, when any member of the group loses his power according to the norms of canon 207, § 1, which regulate the extinguishing of the delegated power, then the power of the entire group suffers the same fate.[26] And although paragraph 3 of this canon does not expressly say so, it is entirely within its wording to maintain that a mere suspension of the power of any one of the group entails likewise a mere suspension of the power of the entire group.[27] Of course this suspension of the power of the group has an invalidating effect, as is clear from canon 205, § 3 since in order to act validly they must act together.

When an alternate provision is made in the concession of collegiate delegation, this fact must be clear from the letter or letters of delegation. This exception to absolute collegiate delegation could be indicated in various ways. The clauses that obtained before the Code are suggested, since they clearly show the intention of the grantor. To cite but one here: *Quod si omnes interesse nequeant, alii eam cognoscant et exsequantur.* The effect of such a clause is the explicit preservation of the collegiate power, despite the deficiency of one member or even a second member.[28]

25 Canon 207, § 3—"Pluribus collegialiter delegatis, si unus deficiat, aliorum quoque delegatio exspirat, nisi aliud ex tenore delegationis constet." Note that the former law required an express provision. Now the "tenor" of the delegation is sufficient to indicate a mitigation of the absolute collegiate character of the delegation. In a case of doubt the delegation is presumed to have been made distributively (*in solidum*) in non-judicial matters, but collegiately (*collegialiter*) in judicial matters (canon 205, § 1).

26 Panormitanus, lib. I, tit. XXIX, c. XVI, n. 3; Pichler, lib. I, tit. XXIX, n. 28; Barbosa, lib. I, tit. XXIX, c. XLII, n. 1; Reiffenstuel, lib. I, tit. XXIX, n. 116; Grandclaude, lib. I, tit. XXIX, § II, n. IV; Wernz, II, n. 561, II; Maroto, I, n. 715a; Coronata, I, n. 290, 7°.

27 Coronata, I, n. 290, 7°.

28 Panormitanus, lib. I, tit. XXIX, c. XXI, n. 1; Reiffenstuel, lib. I, tit. XXIX, n. 119; Wernz, II, n. 557; Bouix, pars 1, n. 150; De Angelis, lib. I, tit. XXIX, n. 7.

Of course, this deficiency must also be authentically established by messenger, letter or witness.[29]

Like the exception just mentioned, other mitigations of absolute collegiate delegation are advanced by canonists. If one of the collegiate delegates whose power is about to expire, or who even foresees that it will be lost, subdelegates another to take his place, the collegiate power does not lapse in the others, since for the deficiency of the one a provision is made through his substitute.[30] The precise examples that could serve for this provision are not indicated by the authors cited; however, according to the principles of delegation, their doctrine is acceptable, posited, of course, the right to subdelegate, and granted also that the subdelegation be limited within the terms of the original delegation.

The second exception suggested by the authors must be accepted with caution, as Kearney wisely suggests.[31] This opinion maintains that the power of the group does not cease if before the loss of power by one of the delegates the matter was undertaken by the whole group.[32] This view is based on the common teaching that delegated power is more firmly founded in the delegate after he begins to exercise the commission. This principle is fully verified even today when applied to a single delegate, but to extend it to an absolute collegiate delegation seems to overlook the fact that this delegated power resides only in the group as such, and could therefore become firmly founded only in the entire group. That a condition relative to the *res integra* could be inserted by the grantor in the letter or letters of delegation is indisputable. But to maintain the perpetuity of a collegiate delegation simply on the basis that the matter is no longer integral appears

[29] Lega-Bartoccetti, I, pp. 201-202.

[30] Cf. Maroto, I, n. 715a; Cocchi, Lib. II, Pars I, p. 247; Wernz, II, n. 561, II; Coronata, I, n. 290, 7°.

[31] Kearney, p. 117.

[32] Maroto, I, n. 715a; Cocchi, Lib. II, Pars I, p. 247; Wernz-Vidal, II, n. 377, 7°, in nota 40.

to the present writer to go beyond the obvious restricted wording of canon 207, § 3.

Moreover, in the supposition that the "tenor" of the delegation does not offer any other indication, the continued exercise of such a delegated power would be futile in view of the invalidating clause of canon 205, § 3. When a delegation is granted collegiately without any mitigating clause, or when the tenor of the delegation does not offer any other indication, then the delegation of its very nature looks not only to a joint activity but also to a total participation, inasmuch as the delegator wills that the complete and entire college execute the matter.[33] If he desires otherwise, the canon invites him to manifest this will.

[33] Cf. Chelodi, n. 129, in nota 5, p. 210; Cappello, *Summa,* I, n. 258, 7°, in nota 12.

CONCLUSIONS

(With Summary of Salient Points)

1. The Roman Law notion of jurisdiction was restricted to judicial matters, and within that restriction served as a forerunner for the canonical usage of the same word. However, the word readily assumed a more extended meaning in ecclesiastical jurisprudence (p. 8).

2. Roman Law made use of the word *delegatio* in a manner entirely distinct from the notion of jurisdiction. This technical usage referred to a contractual relationship whereby a debt was transferred from one person to another (p. 10).

3. The word "delegation" in Roman Law was also used in the sense of judicial power possessed by a delegate, not in his own right or by reason of a proper office of his own, but simply through a mandate or commission from another (p. 12).

4. Decretal Law made abundant use of the groundwork laid down in Roman Law relative to delegated power. It generally reproduced the concepts that were operative during the time of Justinian (pp. 15-16).

5. Delegated power, according to the Code, is that which is directly and fundamentally granted to a person by the commission of another or by disposition of law (p. 17).

6. The regulatory norms established in canon 207 with reference to the cessation of delegated power have direct application only with regard to jurisdictional delegated power; indirectly, through canon 20, they may be applied to all other analogous power (pp. 21-23).

7. The statement that delegated power ceases when the mandate is fulfilled means that both *in causis gratiae* (pp. 32-34) and *in causis iustitiae* (pp. 36-38) the commission must be brought to a valid conclusion. Wherefore, the delegated judge is able to receive the complaint of nullity against his sentence (p. 38). Unless his man-

date so provides, the delegated judge cannot authentically interpret his sentence (pp. 39-40).

8. By reason of the lapse of time for which the delegated power was granted: The cessation of power occurs automatically, independently of any further action by the delegator (p. 42) as in apparent from canon 207, § 1. Nevertheless the delegate may bring to a valid conclusion the matter that was actually undertaken before the time limit had expired, unless an express prohibition to the contrary is inserted in the letter of delegation. Hence the time cannot be extended either by the will of the delegate, much less at the instance of the party or parties (p. 47).

9. By reason of the number of cases for which the delegation was made: The power of the delegate does not cease until each of the number of cases delegated to him has been brought to a valid conclusion (p. 49).

10. Acts of the internal forum which transcend the temporal or numerical restrictions are always valid when the delegate does not advert to the status of his power when he places the act, even though earlier or later he realizes that his power had expired (p. 53). So long as the delegate's inadvertence coincides with the act or acts he performs, his exercise of power is valid, and indeed in virtue of his possession of delegated power, not in virtue of the suppletory norm of canon 209 (pp. 51, 53).

11. Every delegation must have a final cause (p. 56). The delegate's power is not extinguished when the final cause only partially ceases (p. 58). Nor does thc doubtful cessation of the final cause extinguish delegated power (p. 59). The revival of a final cause that had previously ceased must be looked upon as a new final cause, and therefore the delegated power that had also previously ceased cannot automatically revive (p. 59). Whether or not the matter has been jurisdictionally undertaken is irrevelant to this subject (p. 61).

12. Relative to revocation: The act of revocation may

be express or tacit (pp. 65-66), and may be elicited by the delegator, his superior in the direct line of jurisdiction, his successor, or by one designated by any of the aforementioned (pp. 67-68). All acts placed by the delegate or subdelegate prior to the official revocatory intimation by the delegator are valid, since it is the intimation that effectually extinguishes the delegated or the subdelegated power (pp. 69-70). Every delegated power, even though in actual use by the delegate, is subject to the revocatory will of the grantor (p. 70). Subdelegated power follows this same rule, provided the delegate has not abdicated his right by totally transferring his delegated power (p. 74). The revocation of delegated or subdelegated power is always valid, although it may be rendered illicit because of the absence of a just cause (pp. 74-75). Against the revocation there is no appeal, nor any recourse accompanied with a suspensive effect (p. 75).

13. Relative to the words *resoluto iure delegantis*: The general rule maintains the preservation of delegated power despite the physical or legal demise of the grantor (p. 77). There are two exceptions. When a clause, e.g., the proviso of a personal *beneplacitum,* in the rescript of delegation indicates that the sustaining will of the grantor is required, then the delegated power ceases when that grantor loses power (p. 78), even though the delegated matter was undertaken prior to the delegator's demise (pp. 80-82). The word *"et"* in canon 61 refers exclusively to the second exception mentioned therein (p. 81). The second execption refers *only* to a *gratia facienda* or a rescript given *in forma commissoria* with a voluntary executor who is to grant a favor to persons determined in the rescript (p. 82). All other concessions follow the general rule (pp. 83-84). Rescripts of justice follow this general rule of non-cessation, unless the first exception is applicable (pp. 85-86).

14. Concerning renunciation: Prerequisite to the act of renunciation are knowledge and freedom, so that error, force and fear generally must be absent (pp. 95-96). The

act of renunciation may be express or tacit, and may be directed toward every kind of delegated power (pp. 96, 97). The renunciatory will must be officially intimated to the delegator (p. 101). Acceptance of this intimated renunciatory intent is required, and, moreover, to effectively extinguish the power of the delegate, this acceptance by the delegator must be officially brought to the attention of the delegate (pp. 103-106). Acts placed prior to this intimation of acceptance to the delegate are valid in virtue of the delegated power he still possesses (p. 108). The delegate may rightfully seek to renounce his delegated power even after he has begun to use it (pp. 108-109).

15. Relative to the words *resoluto iure delegati*: The provision relative to this factor is not found in canon 207, but rests on the law of nature, the Decretal Law and other places in the Code. Physical death extinguishes the delegate's power (p. 112). His delegated power is lost when he loses the office or dignity on account of which he obtained the delegated power; in this instance the power passes on to the successor in the office or dignity (p. 114). Delegated power is lost by the delegate if he becomes an *excommunicatus vitandus* or is deposed (pp. 116, 119). The cessation of delegated power is not effected by other censures or lesser vindicative penalties although consequent upon the issuance of a declaratory or condemnatory sentence the exercise of jurisdiction is attended with an invalidating effect (pp. 116-119). Delegated power for the handling of a judicial cause is extinguished through a supervening absolute incompetence (p. 121). A sentence which confirms the exception of suspicion against a delegated judge extinguishes his power for the cause in which the exception was raised (pp. 121-123).

16. Concerning delegation given to a group of persons: Multiple delegation presupposes a plurality of passive subjects, delegated in some manner for the same thing (p. 125). The cessation of delegated power which was granted successively to more than one person under canon 206 is

governed by the principles of canon 207, § 1 (p. 127). When delegation is granted to a group in a distributive manner, the loss of delegated power by one does not affect the delegated power of the others (p. 127). The cessation of the power of all who distributively share a delegated power follows the norms of canon 207, § 1 (p. 128). A collegiate delegation, even though no longer integral (*re non amplius integra*), is extinguished in all the members of the college when delegated power is lost by any member of the college according to canon 207, § 1 (p. 129). Two exceptions are sustained, namely, when a clause to the contrary is expressed in the letter or letters of delegation (pp. 129-130), or when one delegate prior to his own demise *legitimately* subdelegates his power to another (p. 130).

BIBLIOGRAPHY

Sources

Acta Apostolicae Sedis, Commentarium Officiale, Romae, 1909——

Acta Sanctae Sedis, 41 vols., Romae, 1865-1908.

Codex Iuris Canonici, Pii X Pontificis Maximi iussu digestus Benedicti Papae XV auctoritate promulgatus, Romae, 1917; Reimpressio, Westminster, Maryland: The Newman Book Shop, 1944.

Codicis Iuris Canonici Fontes, cura Emi Petri Card. Gasparri editi, 9 vols., Romae (postea Civitate Vaticana): Typis Polyglottis Vaticanis, 1923-1939 (Vols. VII-IX, ed. cura et studio Emi Iustiniani Card. Serédi).

Corpus Iuris Canonici, ed. Lipsiensis secunda, post Aemilii Richteri curas... instruxit Aemilius Friedberg, 2 vols., Lipsiae: ex officina Bernhardi Tauchnitz, 1879-1881. Editio anastatice repetita, 1922.

Corpus Iuris Civilis, Vol. I, *Institutiones,* ed. stereotypa 15. recognovit P. Krueger; *Digesta,* ed. stereotypa 15. recognovit T. Mommsen, retractavit P. Krueger; Vol. II, *Codex Iustinianus,* ed. stereotypa 10. recognovit et retractavit P. Krueger; Vol. III, *Novellae Constitutiones,* ed. stereotypa 5. recognovit R. Schoell; opus Schoellii morte interceptum absolvit G. Kroll, Berolini: apud Weidmannos, 1928-1929.

Collectanea Sacrae Congregationis de Propaganda Fide, 2 vols., Romae, 1907.

Decretales D. Gregorii Papae IX, suae integritate una cum Glossis Restitutae, Romae, 1588.

Digestum Vetus, Digestorum seu Pandectarum Iuris Enucleati, adiecimus huic editioni Graecam sanctionem... unaque Francisci Hotomani interpretationem latinam adnotationesque... ex Doctissimorum virorum Commentariis...., Lugduni, 1557.

Institutes of Gaius, Part I, Text with Critical Notes and Translation by Francis de Zulueta, Oxford: At the Clarendon Press, 1946.

Jaffé, Philippus, *Regesta Pontificum Romanorum ab condita Ecclesia ad annum post Christum natum MCXCVIII,* ed. 2. correctam et auctam auspiciis Gulielmi Wattenbach curaverunt S. Loewenfeld, F. Kaltenbrunner, P. Ewald, 2 vols., Lipsiae, 1885-1888.

Potthast, Augustus, *Regesta Pontificum Romanorum inde ab anno post Christum natum MCXCVIII ad annum MCCCIV,* 2 vols., Berolini, 1874-1875.

Sacrae Rotae Romanae Decisiones Nuperrimae, collectio complectens decisiones ab anno MDCLXXXIV usque ad annum MDCCVI, 9 vols. in 10, Romae, 1751-1763.

Schema Codicis Iuris Canonici Sanctissimi Domini Nostri Pii PP. X, cum notis Petri Card. Gasparri, Romae: Typis Polyglottis Vaticanis, 1912.

Reference Works

Aertnys, J., *Theologia Moralis*, 7. ed., 2 vols., Paderbornae, 1906.

Augustine, Charles, *A Commentary on the New Code of Canon Law*, 8 vols., Vol. II, *Clergy and Hierarchy*, 3. ed., St. Louis, Mo.—London, 1919.

Ayrinhac, H. A., *General Legislation in the New Code of Canon Law*, London-New York-Toronto: Longmans, Green and Co., 1933.

Ayrinhac, H. A.-Lydon, P. J., *Penal Legislation in the New Code of Canon Law*, revised ed., New York, Boston, Cincinnati, Chicago, San Francisco: Benziger Brothers, Inc., 1944.

Azo, [The Glossator], *In Ius Civile Summa*, Lugduni, 1564.

Badii, Caesar, *Institutiones Iuris Canonici*, 2 vols., Vol. I, 3. ed., Florentiae, 1921.

Barbosa, Augustinus, *Collectanea Doctorum tam Veterum quam Recentiorum in Jus Pontificium Universum*, 6 vols., Lugduni, 1656.

Bargilliat, M., *Praelectiones Juris Canonici*, 37. ed., ad canones novi Codicis redacta, 2 vols., Parisiis, 1923-1924.

Bartolus a Saxoferrato, *Omnia Opera*, 6. ed., 11 vols., Venetiis, 1590.

Belloni, Joannes, *Tractatus de Mandata Iurisdictione*, Parmae, 1625.

Beste, Udalricus, *Introductio in Codicem*, 3. ed., Collegeville, Minn.: St. John's Abbey Press, 1946.

Blat, Albertus, *Commentarium Textus Codicis Iuris Canonici*, Liber II, *De Personis*, ed. altera, Romae, 1921.

Boich, Henricus, *In Quinque Decretalium Libros Commentaria*, Venetiis, 1576.

Bouix, Dominicus, *Tractatus de Judiciis Ecclesiasticis*, 2 vols. in 1, Parisiis, 1854-1855.

Bouuaert, C.-Simenon, G., *Manuale Juris Canonici*, 3 vols., Vol. I, 5. ed., Gandae et Leodii, 1939.

Brys, J., *Juris Canonici Compendium*, 2 vols., Vol. I, 10. ed. (post Codicem 2[a]), Brugis: Desclée de Brouwer et Sii, 1947.

Buckland, William, *A Text-Book of Roman Law from Augustus to Justinian*, 2. ed., Cambridge, 1932.

Calvinus (Johannes Kahl), *Magnum Lexicon Juridicum*, 2 vols., Coloniae Allobrogum, 1759.

Cappello, Felix, *Summa Iuris Canonici*, 3 vols., Romae: Apud Aedes Universitatis Gregorianae, Vols. I-II, 4. ed., 1945; Vol. III, ed. altera, 1940.

———*Tractatus Canonico-Moralis de Sacramentis*, 5 vols., Augustae Taurinorum Romae: Domus Editorialis Marietti, Vol. II, *De Poenitentia*, 4. ed., 1944; Vol. V, *De Matrimonio*, 5. ed., 1947.

Chelodi, Ioannes, *Ius Canonicum de Personis*, 3. ed. curavit Pius Ciprotti, Trento: Libreria Moderna Editrice, 1942.

Cicognani, Amleto, *Canon Law*, 2. ed., authorized English version by O'Hara-Brennan, Westminster, Maryland: The Newman Press, 1949.

Cocchi, Guidus, *Commentarium in Codicem Iuris Canonici*, 8 vols. in 5, Taurinorum Augustae: Marietti, Liber II, *De Personis*, Pars I, *De Clericis*, 4. ed. recognita, 1937; Liber IV, *De Processibus*, 3. ed. recognita, 1940.

Conrad, Hermann, *Die iurisdictio delegata im römischen und kanonischen Recht*, Inaugural-Dissertation, Köln, 1930.

Coronata, Matthaeus, *Institutiones Iuris Canonici*, 5 vols., Taurini-Romae: Marietti, Vol. I, 3. ed., 1947; Vol. III, ed. altera, 1941; Vol. IV, ed. altera, 1945.

———*Institutiones Iuris Canonici de Sacramentis*, 3 vols., Vol. I, Taurini-Romae: Domus Editorialis Marietti, 1943.

Coyle, Paul R., *Judicial Exceptions*, The Catholic University of America Canon Law Studies, n. 193, Washington, D. C.: The Catholic University of America Press, 1944.

Crisci, Generosus, *De Historia et Doctrina Delegationis a Iure in Iure Romano et Canonico*, Pontificium Institutum Utriusque Iuris Thesis ad Lauream, n. 3, Romae: Apud Custodiam Librariam Pont. Inst. Utriusque Iuris, 1938.

Crnica, Antonius, *Commentarium Theoretico-Practicum Codicis Iuris Canonici*, 2 vols., Šibenik: Typis Typographiae Kačić, 1940-1941.

Cumin, Patrick, *A Manual of Civil Law*, 2. ed., London, 1865.

D'Annibale, J., *Summula Theologiae Moralis*, 3. ed., 3 vols., Romae, 1891-1892.

De Angelis, Philippus, *Praelectiones Juris Canonici ad Methodum Decretalium Gregorii IX Exactae*, 5 vols. in 9, Romae et Parisiis, 1877-1891.

De Meester, A., *Juris Canonici et Juris Canonici-Civilis Compendium*, 3 vols. in 4, Vol. I, ed. nova, Brugis, 1921.

Doheny, William, *Canonical Procedure in Matrimonial Cases, Formal Judicial Procedure*, Milwaukee, Wis.: The Bruce Publishing Company, 1938.

Donellus, Hugo (Doneau, Hugues), *Opera Omnia*, 12 vols., Romae et Maceratae, 1828-1833.

Durandus, Gulielmus, *Speculum Iuris*, 4 vols. in 3, Venetiis, 1577.

Eagleton, George, *The Diocesan Quinquennial Faculties, Formula IV*,

The Catholic University of America Canon Law Studies, n. 248, Washington, D. C.: The Catholic University of America Press, 1948.

Engel, Ludovicus, *Collegium Universi Juris Canonici*, 7. ed., Venetiis, 1733.

Fagnanus, Prosperus, *Commentaria in Quinque Libros Decretalium*, 3 vols., Venetiis, 1709.

Ferraris, Lucius, *Prompta Bibliotheca Canonica, Juridica, Moralis, Theologica, necnon Ascetica, Polemica, Rubricistica, Historica*, ed. novissima, 9 vols., Romae, 1885-1899.

Findlay, Stephen W., *Canonical Norms Governing the Deposition and Degradation of Clerics*, The Catholic University of America Canon Law Studies, n. 130, Washington, D. C.: The Catholic University of America Press, 1941.

Gasparri, Petrus Card., *Tractatus Canonicus de Matrimonio*, 2 vols., ed. nova ad mentem Codicis I. C., Romae: Typis Polyglottis Vaticanis, 1932.

Giraldus, Ubaldus, *Animadversiones et Additamenta ad A. Barbosa de Officio et Potestate Parochi*, Romae, 1831.

Gonzalez-Tellez, Emanuel, *Commentaria Perpetua in Singulos Textus Quinque Librorum Decretalium Gregorii IX*, 5 vols., Lugduni, 1623.

Grandclaude, Eugenius, *Jus Canonicum juxta Ordinem Decretalium*, 3 vols., Parisiis, 1882-1883.

Hostiensis, Cardinalis (Henricus de Segusio), *Summa Aurea*, Venetiis, 1570.

Huth, Adamus, *Jus Canonicum ad Libros V Decretalium Gregorii IX*, Venetiis, 1843.

Hyland, Francis E., *Excommunication, Its Nature, Historical Development and Effects*, The Catholic University of America Canon Law Studies, n. 49, Washington, D. C.: The Catholic University of America, 1928.

Icard, Henri J., *Praelectiones Juris Canonici*, 3 vols., Lutetiae Parisiorum, 1859.

Jone, Heribertus, *Commentarium in Codicem Iuris Canonici*, Vol. I, Paderborn: Officina Libraria F. Schöningh, 1950.

Kearney, Raymond A., *The Principles of Delegation*, The Catholic University of America Canon Law Studies, n. 55, Washington, D. C.: The Catholic University of America, 1929.

Lauer, Arcturus, *Index Verborum Codicis Iuris Canonici*, Romae: Typis Polyglottis Vaticanis, 1941.

Laymann, Paulus, *Theologia Moralis in Quinque Libros Distributa*, 9. ed., Venetiis, 1630.

Lega, Michael-Bartoccetti, Victorius, *Commentarius in Iudicia Ecclesi-*

astica, 3 vols., Romae: Anonima Libraria Cattolica Italiana, 1950.

Lemieux, Delisle A., *The Sentence in Ecclesiastical Procedure*, The Catholic University of America Canon Law Studies, n. 87, Washington, D. C.: The Catholic University of America, 1934.

Leurenius, Petrus, *Jus Canonicum Universum*, 5 vols. in 3, Venetiis, 1729.

Liguori, St. Alphonsus, *Theologia Moralis*, 2 vols., Augustae Taurinorum, 1891.

Maroto, Philippus, *Institutiones Iuris Canonici*, Tomus I, 3. ed., Romae, 1921.

McDevitt, Gerald V., *The Renunciation of an Ecclesiastical Office*, The Catholic University of America Canon Law Studies, n. 218, Washington, D. C.: The Catholic University of America Press, 1946.

Michiels, Gommarus, *Normae Generales Juris Canonici*, ed. altera, 2 vols., Parisiis-Tournaci-Romae: Desclée et Socii, 1949.

Molina, Ludovicus, *De Justitia et Jure, Opera Omnia Tractatibus Quinque*, ed. novissima, 5 vols. in 4, Coloniae Allobrogum, 1759.

Motry, Hubert L., *Diocesan Faculties according to the Code of Canon Law*, The Catholic University of America Canon Law Studies, n. 16, Washington, D. C.: The Catholic University of America, 1922.

Muñiz, T., *Procedimientos Eclesiásticos*, 2. ed., 3 vols., Sevilla: Lib. de Sobrino de Izquierdo, 1926.

Naz, Raoul, *Traité de Droit Canonique*, 4 vols., Paris: Letouzey et Ané, Éditeurs, 1948-1949.

Noone, John, *Nullity in Judicial Acts*, The Catholic University of America Canon Law Studies, n. 297, Washington, D. C.: The Catholic University of America Press, 1950.

Noval, J., *Commentarium Codicis Iuris Canonici*, Lib. IV, *De Processibus*, Augustae Taurinorum, 1920.

Oesterle, Gerardus, *Consultationes de Jure Matrimoniali*, Romae: Officium Libri Catholici, 1942.

———*Praelectiones Iuris Canonici*, Tom. I, Romae: In Collegio S. Anselmi, 1931.

Ojetti, Benedictus, *Commentarium in Codicem Iuris Canonici*, Liber I, *Normae Generales*, Romae, 1927.

———*Synopsis Rerum Moralium et Iuris Pontificii*, 3. ed., 4 vols., Romae, 1909-1914.

O'Neill, William H., *Papal Rescripts of Favor*, The Catholic University of America Canon Law Studies, n. 57, Washington, D. C.: The Catholic University of America, 1930.

Ottaviani, Alaphridus, *Institutiones Iuris Publici Ecclesiastici*, 3. ed., 2 vols., Romae: Typis Polyglottis Vaticanis, 1947-1948.

Panormitanus (Nicholaus de Tudeschis), *Commentaria in Quinque Libros Decretalium,* 5 vols. in 7, Venetiis, 1588.

Passerinus, Petrus, *Commentaria in Sextum Librum Decretalium,* 5 vols. in 2, Venetiis, 1698.

Perez, Antonius, *Opera Omnia,* 4 vols., Romae, 1827.

Pichler, Vitus, *Ius Canonicum secundum Quinque Decretalium Titulos Gregorii Papae IX explicatum,* 2 vols., Ravennae, 1741.

Pirhing, Ernricus, *Jus Canonicum in V Libros Decretalium,* ed. novissima, 5 vols. in 4, Dilingae, 1722.

Poste, E., *Gaii Institutiones or Institutes of Roman Law by Gaius,* Translation and Commentary, 4. ed., revised and enlarged by E. A. Whittuck, Oxford, 1904.

Praeteius, Pardulphus, *Lexicon Iuris Civilis et Canonici,* Francof. ad Moen., 1581.

Prierias, Sylvester, *Summa Sylvestrina,* ed. recens correcta, 2 vols., Venetiis, 1601.

Prince, John E., *The Diocesan Chancellor,* The Catholic University of America Canon Law Studies, n. 167, Washington, D. C.: The Catholic University of America Press, 1942.

Prümmer, Dominicus H., *Manuale Juris Canonici,* ed. 4. et 5., Friburgi Brisgoviae, 1927.

Rainer, Eligius George, *Suspension of Clerics,* The Catholic University of America Canon Law Studies, n. 111, Washington, D. C.: The Catholic University of America, 1937.

Ramstein, Matthew, *A Manual of Canon Law,* Hoboken, N. J.: Terminal Printing and Publishing Co., 1948.

Regatillo, Eduardus, *Ius Sacramentarium,* 2. ed., Santander: Administracion de Sal Terrae, 1949.

———*Institutiones Iuris Canonici,* 2 vols., Santander: Sal Terrae, 1941-1942.

Reiffenstuel, Anacletus, *Jus Canonicum Universum,* 5 vols. in 7, Parisiis, 1864-1870.

Roberti, Franciscus, *De Delictis et Poenis,* Vol. I, Pars II, ed altera, Romae: Apud Custodiam Librariam Pontificii Instituti Utriusque Iuris, 1944.

———*De Processibus,* 2 vols., Vol. I, ed. altera, Romae: Apud Custodiam Librariam Pontificii Instituti Utriusque Iuris, 1941; Vol. II, 1. ed., Romae, 1926.

Roby, Henry J., *Roman Private Law,* 2 vols., Cambridge, 1902.

Roelker, Edward, *Principles of Privileges according to the Code of Canon Law,* The Catholic University of America Canon Law Studies, n. 35, Washington, D. C.: The Catholic University of America, 1926.

Romani, Sylvius, *Institutiones Juris Canonici,* 3 vols., Vol. I, *Jus Constitutionale,* Romae: Via Machiavelli, 1941.

Sanchez, Thomas, *De Sancto Matrimonii Sacramento*, ed. posterior et accuratior, 3 vols. in 1, Venetiis, 1726.

Sandaeus, Felinus, *Commentaria in Quinque Libros Decretalium*, 5 vols. in 3, Venetiis, 1570.

Sanguinetti, Sebastianus, *Iuris Ecclesiastici Institutiones*, 3. ed., Romae, 1896.

Santi, Franciscus-Leitner, Martinus, *Praelectiones Juris Canonici*, 3. ed., 5 vols. in 4, Ratisbonae-Romae-Neo Eboraci-Cincinnati, 1903-1905.

Schmalzgrueber, Franciscus, *Jus Ecclesiasticum Universum*, 5 vols. in 12, Romae, 1843-1845.

Schmidt, John Rogg, *The Principles of Authentic Interpretation in Canon 17 of the Code of Canon Law*, The Catholic University of America Canon Law Studies, n. 141, Washington, D. C.: The Catholic University of America Press, 1941.

Schulz, Fritz, *Principles of Roman Law*, translated by Marguerite Wolff, Oxford: The Clarendon Press, 1936.

Sebastianelli, Gulielmus, *Praelectiones Juris Canonici, De Personis*, 2. ed., Romae, 1905.

Sherman, Charles F., *Roman Law in the Modern World*, 2. ed., 3 vols., New York, 1924.

Sohm, Rudolf, *The Institutes, A Textbook of the History and System of Roman Private Law*, 3. ed., translated by James Ledlie, Oxford, 1907.

Strykius, Samuel, *Opera Omnia*, 8 vols., Frankofurti et Lipsiae, 1743.

Suarez, Franciscus, *Opera Omnia*, ed. nova, 28 vols., Parisiis, 1856-1861.

Thomas Aquinas, St., *Opera Omnia*, Vivés edition, 34 vols., Parisiis, Vol. XII, *Summa Contra Gentiles*, 1874; Vol. XXVII, *Opuscula Varia* (*De Principiis Naturae*, pp. 480-486, *De Regimine Principum*, pp. 336-338), 1899.

Toso, Albertus, *Ad Codicem Juris Canonici... Commentaria Minora*, 2 Lib. in 5 Tom., Lib. I, *Normae Generales*, 2. ed., Taurini- Romae: Marietti, 1921; Lib. II, *De Personis*, Tom. I, Taurini-Romae: Marietti, 1922.

Van Hove, A., *Commentarium Lovaniense in Codicem Iuris Canonici*, Mechliniae-Romae: H. Dessain, Vol. I, Tom. IV, *De Rescriptis*, 1936; Vol. I, Tom. V, *De Privilegiis-De Dispensationibus*, 1939.

Vermeersch, A.-Creusen, J., *Epitome Iuris Canonici*, 3 vols., Mechliniae-Romae: H. Dessain, Vol. I, 7. ed., 1949; Vol. II, 6. ed., 1940; Vol. III, 6. ed., 1946.

Veranus, Cajetanus F., *Juris Canonici Universi Commentarius Paratitlaris*, 5 vols., Monachii, 1703-1708.

Voet, J., *Ad Pandectas*, 5. ed., 7 vols. in 4, Bassani, 1827.

Vromant, G., *Ius Missionariorum—Facultates Apostolicae quas Sacra Congregatio de Propaganda Fide delegare solet Ordinariis Missionum,* ed. 3. emendata, Paris: Desclée De Brouwer, 1947.

Warnkoenig, Leopold A., *Institutiones Iuris Romani Privati,* 4. ed., Bonn, 1860.

Wenger, Leopold, *Institutes of the Roman Law of Civil Procedure,* revised ed., translated by Otis Harrison Fisk, New York: Veritas Press, 1940.

Wernz, Franciscus, *Ius Decretalium,* 6 vols., Vol. II, *Ius Constitutionis Ecclesiae Catholicae,* 3. ed., Prati, 1915; Vol. VI, *Ius Poenale Ecclesiae Catholicae,* 1. ed., Prati, 1913.

Wernz, F.-Vidal, P., *Ius Canonicum,* 7 vols. in 8, Romae: Apud Aedes Universitatis Gregorianae, Tom. II, *De Personis,* ed. 3. a Philippo Aguirre recognita, 1943; Tom. VI, *De Processibus,* ed. altera a Felice M. Cappello recognita, 1949.

Woywod, Stanislaus, *A Practical Commentary on the Code of Canon Law,* 2 vols., 8. printing, revised by C. Smith, New York: Joseph F. Wagner—London: B. Herder, 1944.

PERIODICALS

Ephemerides Iuris Canonici, Romae, 1945—

Irish Ecclesiastical Record, The, Dublin, 1864—

Jurist, The, Washington, D. C., 1941—

Jus Pontificium, Romae, 1921-1940.

ARTICLES

———"S. R. Rota Sententia Recentiores," *Ephemerides Iuris Canonici,* II (1946), 347-352.

Bastnagel, C., "Temporal Limits for Revoking Resignation from Office," *The Jurist,* IX (1949), 408-412.

———"Authorization of the Further Committing of Subdelegated Power," *The Jurist,* IX (1949), 412-414.

Galassi, Italus, "De delegatione ad matrimonio assistendum," *Ephemerides Iuris Canonici,* II (1946), 347-352.

Kinane, J., "Jurisdiction in the New Code," *The Irish Ecclesiastical Record,* 5. series, XIII (1919), 204-218.

Van de Kerckhove, M., "De Notione Jurisdictionis apud Decretistas et Priores Decretalistas," *Jus Pontificium,* XVIII (1938), 10-14.

———"De Notione Jurisdictionis in Jure Romano," *Jus Pontificium,* XVI (1936), 49-65.

Roelker, E., "An Introduction to the Rules of Law," *The Jurist,* X (1950), 417-436.

Abbreviations

AAS—*Acta Apostolicae Sedis.*
C.—*Codex Iustinianus.*
D.—*Digesta* (*Iustiniana*).
Fontes—*Codicis Iuris Canonici Fontes.*
Inst.—*Institutiones* (*Iustinianae*).
Jaffé—*Regesta Pontificum Romanorum . . . ad annum MCXCVIII.*
Nuperrimae—*Sacrae Rotae Romanae Decisiones Nuperrimae.*
Potthast—*Regesta Pontificum Romanorum . . . ad annum MCCCIV.*
R. J.—*Regula Juris.*
Schema C. I. C.—*Schema Codicis Iuris Canonici.*

BIOGRAPHICAL NOTE

Max George DeWitt was born September 17, 1923, in Hastings, Nebraska. He received his elementary and high school education from St. Cecilia's Parochial School in that city. In September, 1941, he began preparatory studies for the priesthood at St. John's Home Mission Seminary in Little Rock, Arkansas, from which he received the degree of Bachelor of Arts in February of 1945. He was then transferred to St. Francis Major Seminary in Milwaukee, Wisconsin, where he made the courses in Theology. Ordination to the Holy Priesthood followed on May 6, 1948. After a year of parochial duties in the Diocese of Lincoln, he was enrolled in the School of Canon Law at the Catholic University of America. At the end of the 1949-1950 scholastic year he received the degree of the Baccalaureate in Canon Law. The degree of the Licentiate in Canon Law he received at the close of the 1950-1951 scholastic year.

ALPHABETICAL INDEX

CANON LAW STUDIES*

327. Koesler, Rev. Leo J., O.S.B., J.C.L., Entrance into the Novitiate by Clerics in Major Orders (Canon 542, 2°).
328. McFarland, Rev. Norman E., J.C.L., Essential Conditions and Sufficient Signs of Vocation to the Religious Life.
329. Wiest, Rev. Donald Herman, O.F.M.Cap., S.T.B., J.C.L., The Precensorship of Books.
330. De Witt, Rev. Max George, A.B., J.C.L., The Cessation of Delegated Power.
331. Mathis, Rev. Marcian John, O.F.M., J.C.D., The Constitution and Supreme Administration of Regional Seminaries Subject to the Sacred Congregation for the Propagation of the Faith in China.
332. Schorr, Rev. George F., A.B., J.C.D., The Law of the Celebret.
333. Sheehy, Rev. Robert Francis, A.B., J.C.L., The Sacred Congregation of the Sacraments: Its Competence in the Roman Curia.
334. Shields, Rev. Joseph A., A.B., J.C.L., Deprivation of the Clerical Garb.
335. Uricheck, Rev. George Edward, A.B., J.C.L., De forma celebrationis matrimonii in Ecclesiis Orientalibus ante Motu Proprio *Crebrae Allatae* et post.
336. De Pauw, Rev. Gommar A., J.C.L., The Legal Status of Catholic Elementary Schools in Belgium, 1830-1950.

www.ingramcontent.com/pod-product-compliance
Lightning Source LLC
LaVergne TN
LVHW050224080826
844660LV00012B/465

* 9 7 8 0 8 1 3 2 2 5 0 1 2 *